the
MIRACLE
JUICE
diet

the MIRACLE JUICE diet

LOSE 3 KG (7 LBS) IN JUST 7 DAYS!

AMANDA CROSS

hamlyn

An Hachette Livre UK Company

First published in Great Britain in 2008 by
Hamlyn, a division of Octopus Publishing Group Ltd,
2–4 Heron Quays, London E14 4JP
www.octopusbooks.co.uk

Distributed in the United States and Canada by
Sterling Publishing Co., Inc.
387 Park Avenue South, New York, NY 10016-8810

ISBN 978-0-600-61708-2

A CIP catalogue record for this book is available from the
British Library

Printed and bound in China

10 9 8 7 6 5 4 3 2 1

NOTES
Both metric and imperial measurements are given for the recipes. Use
one set of measures only, not a mixture of both.

DISCLAIMER
This book is meant to be used as a general reference and recipe guide to
aid weight loss. However, you are urged to consult a health-care
professional to check whether it is a suitable weight-loss plan for you,
before embarking on it.

While all reasonable care has been taken during the preparation of this
edition, neither the publishers, editors nor the author can accept
responsibility for any consequences arising from the use of this
information.

Notes for American readers

Ingredients: equivalents and substitutions

UK	US
aubergine	eggplant
beetroot	beet
calamari	squid
coriander	cilantro
courgette	zucchini
crudités	raw vegetables
green-lipped mussels	greenshell mussels
mangetout	snow pea
marrow	squash
natural yogurt	plain yogurt
pak choi	bok choy
papaya	pawpaw
pepper, red/green/yellow	bell pepper
pink grapefruit	ruby grapefruit
prawns	shrimp
pumpkin seed	pepitas
rocket	arugula
root ginger	ginger root
spring onion	scallion
soya	soy
wholemeal	whole wheat

Approximate conversions

60 ml (2 fl oz)	$^{1}/_{4}$ US cup
120 ml (4 fl oz)	$^{1}/_{2}$ US cup
180 ml (6 fl oz)	$^{3}/_{4}$ US cup
240 ml (8 fl oz)	1 US cup
1 litre (1$^{3}/_{4}$ UK pints)	4 US cups

Some standard equivalents

The following are the equivalent of 1 US cup:
125 g (4 oz) flour /
225 g (8 oz) granulated or caster (superfine) sugar
125 g (4 oz) icing (confectioners') sugar
225 g (8 oz) butter
200 g (6 oz) rice

Contents

Introduction 6

1   the science behind the diet 8

2   getting physical 30

3   pre-diet plan 42

4   the diet 56

5   making the diet work for you 100

Index 110

Acknowledgements 112

Introduction

I would bet that what prompted you to buy this book was the statement 'lose up to **3 kg (7 lb)** in **7 days**'. Well, it's not a fake promise. You can. Whether you want to fit into a special outfit, **look great** on the beach or kick-start a long-term weight plan, one week on the diet will help you **achieve** your goal.

It will also leave you feeling cleaner and more energized, as not only does it help you lose unwanted pounds, it will start to help your body rid itself of toxins that make you feel lethargic and set you up for a whole host of chronic conditions and diseases. Even if you are treating this as a quick fix solution to a long-term weight problem, you will lose the pounds and give your body a holiday from all your usual bad habits. Hopefully, you'll come out the other side sufficiently inspired to improve your diet and clean up your act on a more permanent basis.

But remember – this will take determination. Making juices and smoothies five times a day takes a lot more effort than throwing something in the microwave or ordering in a pizza. If you haven't got a juicer and a blender already, this means a little investment on your part. And even though this diet isn't as extreme as other 'fruit-and-vegetable' fasts, it is still a powerful detox, and you will need to make preparations so that this diet is as safe and effective as possible.

Read on; even if you are tempted to skip the information at the beginning of the book and go straight to the diet plan, please don't. It is important that you understand the impact this diet plan will have on your body and follow the advice regarding the days leading up to the diet and exercising during that period.

Equally important is the advice on page 106 on how you should reintroduce food into your diet after your week on juices is up. I have taken into consideration how difficult a regime like this can be for busy people and have allowed for adaptations that may not produce such a dramatic weight loss result, but will nevertheless allow you to lose weight steadily and revitalize your body.

Along with the dietary advice, I have suggested an exercise regime that will kick-start your metabolism and strengthen your body, as well as giving tips on how to make sure your seven-day experience is as holistically beneficial as possible.

So get ready to fill your refrigerator with masses of healthy vitamin- and mineral-packed fruits and vegetables and begin your juicing journey. Destination – 3 kg (7 lb) lighter.

What are you waiting for? Remember, the only person holding you back is you!

the science
behind the diet

how does the diet work?

Ever done a spring clean? Gone through every cupboard and room in the house **chucking out** accumulated **clutter?** Think of how much 'lighter' you felt when you were done.

Your body works in a similar way. Many people carry excess weight because their systems are weighted down with an overload of toxins from poor diets and the pollutants we face daily. Added to which, if you don't drink enough water, your body retains fluid in an attempt to dilute these toxins and support your vital organs. The result? Weight gain.

the fat factor

According to recent studies by the US Environmental Protection Agency, over 400 chemicals have been found in human tissue – the majority of which are found in the blood, the liver and adipose tissue – commonly known as fat.

how does this affect your weight?

Let's look at basic biology. Various systems in your body work together to keep you 'on the road' and functioning, and to do this, they all need fuel. When the quality of the fuel (air, water and food) is contaminated, they have to work even harder, because the body has no natural mechanism to deal with man-made toxins.

Initially, the major responsibility rests with the liver. If the liver is over-taxed and unsupported by the right sort of nutrients, something has got to give, so the job goes to the excretory system. If the kidneys can't deal with the deluge of toxins in the blood, they send the toxins via the lymphatic system to a safe storage unit to your fat cells.

The more toxins your body has to deal with, the more fat cells it needs to store them, so a vicious cycle begins. As the body is burdened with more waste products, the slower your metabolism becomes, which can make losing weight a difficult task.

This diet works because it eliminates toxins in two ways: by cleansing your system and then nourishing it, so that you get a cleaner, slimmed down body fast!

cleansing

Juices have a very high water content, so they 'sweep' through your body fast, hydrating the cells and helping your kidneys and lymphatic system to rid it of accumulated waste and toxins that create the fluid retention and make you sluggish and bloated. It also helps to improve elimination from the colon and prevents the re-absorption of toxins back into the system.

nourishing

The juice and smoothie recipes, along with the snacks and supplements in the plan, are specifically designed to support and reinforce your systems with a super-charged cocktail of nutrients essential for health and vitality (see pages 18–19 for more about vital nutrients). When you juice, your machine takes all the hard work out of digestion as it extracts the fibre from the fruits and vegetables. This allows their health-boosting nutrients to be absorbed immediately by the body. Your system can function more efficiently, improving your metabolism and speeding up weight loss (see page 12).

It's important on any diet to consume enough calories. Too few and your body, programmed for survival, will think that it needs to protect itself from starvation and will store energy in the form of fat. This diet is designed so that you get just the right number of calories to ensure that you have all the energy you need for daily life and enable you to lose weight.

benefits of the juicing diet

Some people will look at this diet and dismiss it as some kind of **dangerous fast**. The very same people probably drink copious amounts of coffee and alcohol, have **erratic eating** habits and fill themselves with **unhealthy foods** that deplete rather than nourish their bodies.

Fasting generally means that you are abstaining from food, thus denying your body any form of nutrition. All the juices in this diet are full of vital nutrients that support your system and supply sufficient calories to provide your body with enough energy to maintain your daily commitments. They also taste fantastic, so you're not exactly depriving yourself.

The main benefits are the high vitamin and mineral content and the presence of essential phytonutrients and amino acids that ensure optimum health. They also contain vital enzymes that are responsible for digestion and absorption of food into your body, converting foods into body tissue and enabling the production of energy. Without such enzymes your metabolism cannot function at its optimal rate. Enzymes cannot exist at temperatures higher than 114°C (237°F), so cooking destroys many of these important nutrients.

The single most effective way to take in as many of these enzymes as possible is to eat the majority of your fruits and vegetables raw.

why juice?

Have you ever tried to eat a whole bag of carrots? Juicing good-quality fresh fruits and vegetables gives you a super boost of nutrients that are easily assimilated by the body as you have taken away the majority of the fibre that slows down this process. By treating your body to these highly nutritious cocktails, you will feel more satisfied for longer than you would if you had eaten, say, a chocolate bar high in refined sugar and unhealthy fats, that will leave your body craving for more after the initial sugar rush has worn off.

but don't we need fibre?

Of course we need fibre and you will be taking in fibre on the seven-day plan: firstly in the form of soluble fibre that juicing doesn't remove; and secondly, in the recommended daily fibre supplement through flax seeds and psyllium husks (see pages 24–5). This is more effective as the essential nutrients are separate from the fibre source and remain immediately available to nourish the tissues and cells of the body.

can't I just buy ready-made juice from the supermarket?

Many commercially available juices and smoothies have been diluted with water, heat-treated and may contain additives to prolong their shelf life, thus minimizing their nutritional benefit. It is best to make your own or go to a juice bar where juices can be made to your specification with fresh ingredients right there in front of you. Alternatively, if you are stuck, seek out good-quality juices and smoothies from the chiller cabinet.

Remember that this is a seven-day plan; on a more long-term basis, supplementing a healthy diet with freshly squeezed juices and smoothies will ensure you receive your daily minimum quota of five portions of fruit and vegetables and help provide all the key nutrients you need for maintaining vibrant health.

the detox bonus

There are no two ways about it, we live in a toxic world; whether it's **external pollution**, abusing our bodies with a **poor diet** or leading too stressful lives, we are all vulnerable.

By embarking on this diet, you are not only helping your body shed unwanted pounds, you are also giving your system a chance to detox. By the end of seven days you could experience restored vitality, more mental clarity, clearer skin and eyes and a strengthened immune system, which means you'll be looking and feeling healthy in every aspect of your being. By detoxifying your body, you can enjoy these benefits and more.

Practised for centuries by many cultures around the world – including Ayurvedic and Chinese medicine systems – detoxification involves resting, cleansing and nourishing the body from the inside out. By eliminating toxins, then feeding your body with healthy nutrients, detoxifying can help protect you from disease and renew your ability to maintain optimum health.

how does detoxification work?

Basically, detoxification means cleansing the blood. It does this mainly by removing impurities from the blood in the liver, where toxins are processed for elimination. The body also eliminates toxins through the kidneys, colon, lungs, lymph and skin. However, when this system is compromised, impurities aren't properly filtered and every cell in the body is adversely affected. Degenerative disease usually springs from either one or a combination of two main conditions: deficiency – not enough nutrients being taken in, or congestion – an excess of toxins from an unhealthy lifestyle.

So cleansing and nourishing the system is vital to the body for overall health. It helps with weight control as it supports two very important organs.

the liver

Your liver is your body's filter. It has the difficult task of neutralizing many subtances that your body either produces as a result of normal metabolism or comes into contact with. If your liver becomes bogged down with toxins it cannot metabolize ingested fats properly, so dumps them straight back into the bloodstream along with an unhealthy dose of cholesterol. This not only plays havoc with your health, it sabotages weight-loss attempts.

the colon

Your colon is designed to eliminate body waste along with toxins. The great thing about this diet plan is that it provides the body with masses of enzymes that enable the liver to do its detoxifying job and aid elimination by breaking down and liquefying food in the digestive tract, augmented by an abundance of vitamins and minerals, without which the enzymes couldn't do their good work.

vitamins, minerals & antioxidants

The work of minerals and vitamins is interrelated and each helps the other to be **absorbed** and **utilized**. So a diet rich in both is essential, particularly when on a weight loss and detoxification regime.

Vitamins are vital to human nutrition and can only be found in living things, that is, plants and animals. Specific combinations of these nutrients, in conjunction with other substances such as minerals and phytonutrients, ensure that all bodily systems function correctly. If the diet is lacking then supplementation is essential. This is often the case when a person eats nutritionally depleted food, not enough food or is putting extra pressure on the body through overwork, during illness or following surgery or when you are undergoing high levels of stress.

fat-soluble vitamins

There are two types of vitamins – fat-soluble and water-soluble. When you eat foods that contain fat-soluble vitamins, the vitamins are stored in the fat tissues in your body and in your liver, ready to be utilized when your body needs them. Vitamins A, D, E and K are all fat-soluble vitamins.

water-soluble vitamins

Water-soluble vitamins are different. When you eat foods that contain water-soluble vitamins, they can't be stored in your body. Instead, they travel through your bloodstream and any excess is expelled in the urine. This group of vitamins includes vitamin C and the big group of B vitamins – B1 (thiamin), B2 (riboflavin), niacin, B6 (pyridoxine), folic acid, B12 (cobalamine), biotin and pantothenic acid.

minerals

Minerals are nutrients that exist in the body and in food in organic and inorganic combinations. Approximately 17 minerals have been found to be essential to human nutrition. Roughly four to five per cent of human body weight is mineral matter. They are vital to overall health and physical wellbeing. All tissues and internal fluids of living things contain varying amounts of minerals, and they are also the major constituents of the bones, teeth, soft tissue, muscle, blood and nerve cells.

There is a clear and important distinction between the terms 'mineral' and 'trace element'. If the body requires more than 100 mg of a mineral each day, the substance is labelled mineral. If the body requires less than 100 mg of a mineral each day, the substance is labelled a trace element.

Minerals are fundamental to maintaining the delicate water balance essential to mental and physical processes. They keep blood and tissue fluids at their correct pH balance and facilitate the passing of other nutrients into the bloodstream. They also help to draw chemical substances in and out of the cells and aid the creation of antibodies. On this diet, care has been taken and advice given to ensure that the full spectrum of vitamins and minerals is part of the daily intake.

phytonutrients

Until recently, it was thought that fats, proteins, carbohydrates, vitamins and minerals were all the **nutrients necessary** for growth and health. Now we know there's **another group** of nutrients necessary for **optimal health** – phytonutrients (from Greek *phyton* meaning 'plant').

Molecular science is finally confirming that the power-packed nutrients that give fruits and vegetables their many colours also provide a lot of Mother Nature's medicine. While many phytonutrients have been identified, there are probably thousands more that remain undiscovered.

Phytonutrients protect the body and fight disease. They help the cells repair themselves by stimulating the release of protective enzymes or those that rebuild damaged cells. This makes them essential in the fight against cancer. Carcinogens (cancer-causing substances) can enter the body from many sources: tobacco smoke, pollution, pesticides and chemicals from many manufactured products. Once in the body these carcinogens can create disease. Phytonutrients inhibit cancer-producing substances, reducing their ability to damage cells. When the repair squad can stay ahead of the damage, degenerative diseases such as cancer, multiple sclerosis and arthritis can't get started. Antioxidant phytonutrients also keep cardiovascular disease in check by blocking the damaging effects of LDL cholesterol on arteries.

the significance of the Mediterranean diet

This phyto-protective mechanism explains why cultures whose diets are rich in plant foods have the lowest rates of cancer and heart disease. The Mediterranean diet, for example, emphasizes garlic, tomatoes, onions, fruits, whole grains and olive oil – all of which are rich in phytonutrients.

It's not only what fruits and vegetables contain that make them effective cancer-fighters; it's also what they don't contain – saturated and hydrogenated fats, refined sugar and grains, and chemical pollutants frequently found in processed foods.

Whereas a huge amount of information exists about vitamins, phytonutrients are newcomers to the health-food table. The 'pill-pushers' try to sell them as supplements, even though the medical world is still trying to establish their exact role. So if you find the information confusing, follow a few 'phyto-rules'.

* Like other nutrients, phytonutrients operate under the biochemical principle of synergy (1 + 1 = 3). For example, flavonoids and carotenoids have more health-promoting properties when they are eaten together in the same food rather than when they are taken separately in a health supplement. By eating a few florets of broccoli you're not only getting the beta-carotene you could get in a pill, but you're probably also getting the health benefits of hundreds or thousands of other phytonutrients that don't even have names yet. And, of course, you're getting all the other nutrients too.
* Each class of phytonutrients affects cellular wellbeing differently and the greatest way to take full advantage of the best medicine nature has to offer is to eat a variety of fruits and vegetables.
* Raw vegetables have more nutrients than cooked ones.

PHYTONUTRIENTS AND THEIR BENEFITS

PHYTONUTRIENTS	PLANT	BENEFITS
Allyl sulphide	Garlic and onions	Allicin in these vegetables is a potent antiviral and antibacterial agent. Decreases the risk of stomach and colon cancer, lowers LDL (bad cholesterol), encourages production of the enzyme glutathione S-transferase, which helps eliminate toxins from the body
Lutein	Green leafy vegetables, spinach, turnip, beet tops, spring greens, kale, yellow marrow and squash	This carotene antioxidant protects against degenerative diseases, including macular degeneration. Also protects all body cells from premature ageing
Indoles, sulphoraphanes	Broccoli, Brussels sprouts, cabbage, other leafy green vegetables	Indoles eliminate toxins, enhance immunity and prevent cancer-causing hormones from attaching themselves to cells. Sulphoraphanes remove carcinogens from cells
Isoflavones such as saponins, phytosterols, genistein	Soya products, cruciferous vegetables, cucumber, sweet potatoes, tomatoes	Isoflavones are powerful antioxidants that protect against cancer. Genistein prevents the body taking up dangerous chemical oestrogens. Saponins enhance immune functions and help to prevent absorption of cholesterol. Phytosterols lower cholesterol
Lycopene, P-coumaric acid, coumarins	Tomatoes, tomato juice, watermelon, pink grapefruit, papaya, oranges, mango	From the same family as beta-carotene, lycopene has great antioxidant power and guards against colon and bladder cancer and reduces risk of cardiovascular disease. P-coumaric acid (also found in strawberries and red peppers) inhibits the production of cancer causing nitrosamines in the body. Coumarins reduce inflammation
Limonene, glucarase	Citrus fruits: oranges, tangerines, grapefruits	Limonene enhances immunity and increases production of anti-cancer enzymes. Glucarase eliminates degenerative chemicals from the body
Alpha-carotene, beta-carotene (carotenoids)	Orange vegetables and fruits: mangos, pumpkins, carrots, sweet potatoes, squash, marrows	Antioxidants with a huge ability to boost immunity and decrease risk of many cancers, degenerative disease and ageing
Polyphenols, flavonoids, anthocyanins	Berries, red grapes, red wine, artichokes, yams	These lower the risk of heart disease, flush out chemicals. Flavonoids fight cell damage from oxidation, strengthen blood vessels and capillaries, improve skin and eyesight
Lignan precursors	Flax seeds or linseeds	Lignan precursors help prevent cancer and are great sources of omega-3 fatty acids

top 20 fruit & vegetables

This **top 20** is filled with vitamins, minerals and phytonutrients by the score. **Mix** them up and eat some of **each colour** every day.

1 melons are highly nutritious and many melons are natural diuretics, so are also powerful cleansers and detoxifiers. Because of their high water content they are also great for rehydration. Orange melons such as cantaloupe are high in beta-carotene. Watermelons have anticoagulant properties and all melons are antiviral and antibacterial.

2 kiwifruit are packed with vitamin C and full of fibre. They contain actinidin, an enzyme that is excellent for the immune system, lowering blood pressure and all-round heart health. They were known as Chinese gooseberries and are revered in traditional Chinese medicine for their healing effect on stomach and breast cancer.

3 bananas are one of the best sources of potassium, an essential mineral for maintaining normal blood pressure and heart function. A banana a day may help to prevent high blood pressure and protect against atherosclerosis. The fibre content helps to prevent cardiovascular disease and the calcium content helps to promote bone health. Bananas contain pectin, a soluble fibre (called a hydrocolloid) that can help normalize movement through the digestive tract and ease constipation. Bananas are an exceptionally rich source of prebiotics that nourish probiotic (friendly) bacteria in the colon. These beneficial bacteria produce vitamins and digestive enzymes that improve our ability to absorb nutrients, plus compounds that protect us against unfriendly micro-organisms, and gastrointestinal transit time is lessened, decreasing the risk of colon cancer.

4 berries of all kinds do so much for our general health. Fill your freezer with red and purple nutritious berries when fresh are not in season. They are antiviral and antibacterial. Berries of all sorts are fabulous for the bloodstream. Blueberries and blackcurrants help diarrhoea and any urinary infection. Raspberries contain natural aspirin and are reputedly good for menstrual cramps. Strawberries are high in pectin, full of lycopene and benefit the cardiovascular system as a whole.

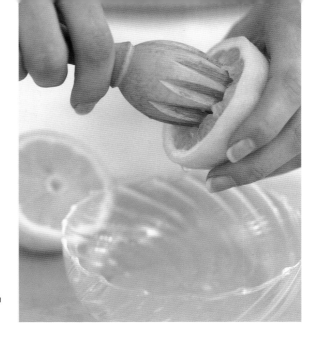

5 **avocados** are a complete food, packed with essential nutrients. They lower blood cholesterol and contain glutathione, which blocks 30 different carcinogens. The high vitamin E content is excellent for maintaining a healthy skin, healing wounds and bolstering the immune system. They are also a good source of lecithin, which helps the body digest and metabolize fats.

6 **cranberries** deodorize urine and prevent bacteria in the bladder, prostate and kidneys. They have the power to keep the entire urinary tract free from infection as they contain mannose, which is more effective than antibiotics. Cranberries can also help prevent kidney stones and are antiviral and antibiotic. They are very sour and may need to be combined with sweeter fruit in juices and smoothies.

7 **citrus fruits**, collectively oranges, lemons, limes and grapefruits contain carotenoids, bioflavonoids and huge levels of vitamin C that are key in the fight against cancer. They lower blood cholesterol and arterial plaque. Citrus fruits are antiviral, antibacterial and extremely versatile, since they give a great burst of flavour to any juice or smoothie.

8 **papaya** is the tops when it comes to aiding digestion as it contains the enzyme papain, which helps to break down protein. It protects against cancer and replenishes lost levels of vitamin C, making it a very good choice for smokers.

9 **apples** are antioxidants, reduce cholesterol, cleanse the digestive system and boost the immune system. Apples provide an excellent base for many juices, and even a small addition of apple will soften the taste of a stronger vegetable blend. Apples are also full of nutrients that aid in the digestion of fats.

10 **plums** are full of phenols and are powerful antioxidants. They help increase absorption of iron into the body and are a great source of vitamin C, so are a good immune-boosting choice of fruit. Plums are a good source of vitamin A (in the form of beta-carotene), vitamin B2, dietary fibre and potassium.

11 **pineapples** add fantastic flavour to many juices and smoothies. They are anti-inflammatory, antiviral and antibacterial. They are able to help dissolve blood clots and contain the digestive enzyme bromelain, which is essential in the digestion of protein.

12 **mangos** are mighty impressive, self-contained packages of vitamins, minerals and antioxidants. Mango is a shining star in the beta-carotene realm and is full of potassium. It's the perfect fruit to replenish energy after heavy physical exercise like jogging or working out.

13 **tomatoes** have got to be the most versatile ingredient known to man and so fantastic for our health. They lower the risk of cancer and heart disease due to the presence of lycopene, which fights off free radicals. Tomatoes mix well with most other fruits and vegetables.

14 **broccoli** is a member of the cruciferous family of vegetables. These are loaded with antioxidants and broccoli is pulsating with vitamin C. It is vital to have a regular intake of this vegetable if you want to guard against lung, breast and colon cancer. On a low carb regime, broccoli is useful as it helps to regulate insulin and blood sugar. It has been reported that it can even deactivate cancer cells.

15 **cabbage** is a leading cancer fighter. It is full of indoles, can regulate oestrogen metabolism and discourage formation of polyps. Cabbage is definitely best eaten raw and ideally should be included in the diet two or three times a week. As a detoxifier it is massively effective and it is a great ingredient in juices. The downside? The taste. But if you mix it with more pleasant-tasting fruits and vegetables, the juice can actually be very palatable.

16 **sweet potatoes** contain unique root storage proteins that have significant antioxidant capacities. Because of their high level of carotenoids they also help stabilize blood sugar levels and lower insulin resistance. An excellent source of vitamin A (in the form of beta-carotene), a very good source of vitamin C and manganese, and a good source of copper, dietary fibre, vitamin B6, potassium and iron. Since these nutrients are also anti-inflammatory, they can be helpful in reducing the severity of conditions where inflammation plays a role, such as asthma, rheumatoid arthritis and osteoarthritis.

17 **peppers** are rich in vitamin C and have antioxidant properties. They help guard against macular degeneration and respiratory infections. They also help to keep arteries decongested and are said to be effective in helping conditions such as asthma, bronchitis and even the common cold. Peppers are rich in natural silicones, which help to keep nails, skin and hair glossy and healthy.

18 **green leafy vegetables** should be an integral part of the daily diet. Spinach, kale, spring greens, pak choi are all rich in antioxidants, full of lutein and beta-carotene and will battle cancer and regulate oestrogen. Even if you favour sweeter fruit-based juices, try to have a couple of green juices per week. Your system will thank you for it and glowing health can be yours.

19 **celery and fennel** are all great at cleansing the digestive system of uric acid. They have a high potassium content and are therefore great for lowering high blood pressure. If you hold on to excess fluid and suffer from regular bloating, their diuretic effect is very powerful and if you wish to detoxify your body, these should be the basis of the juices you create.

20 **carrots** when cooked rate very highly on the carb scale, less when they are raw, and are too good a juicing ingredient to miss out. Used carefully and moderately carrots are nutritional power houses. Their antioxidant capabilities stem from a very high beta-carotene content. They fight cancer, protect arteries, battle infections and boost immunity. They are said to eliminate putrefactive bacteria in the colon and facilitate elimination of intestinal parasites. Carrots are also effective against macular degeneration and blend well with virtually all other ingredients.

supplements
& super foods

Even though this is a week-long programme based on an abundance of vitamins, minerals and **health-enhancing** phytonutrients, you will need to take a few things alongside your delicious juices and **smoothies** in order to maintain a healthy balance.

flax

Flax seeds and flax oil are being rediscovered as true health foods. It is recommended to have a daily tablespoon of flax oil or 2 tablespoons of flax seed meal. Besides being the best vegetarian source of ALA omega-3, flax oil is a good source of omega-6 or linoleic acid (LA). But on this regime I advise having flax seeds as they contain other nutrients that make eating the whole seed superior to consuming just the extracted oil: a high-quality protein, soluble fibre (the combination of the oil and the fibre makes flax seeds an ideal laxative), vitamins B1, B2, C, E and carotene, iron, zinc and trace amounts of potassium, magnesium, phosphorus and calcium. Flax seeds are high in the phytonutrient lignan. Lignans flush excess oestrogen from the body, thereby reducing the incidence of oestrogen-linked cancers, such as breast cancer. Besides their anti-tumour properties, lignans are also antibacterial, antifungal and antiviral.

Foods high in essential fatty acids, such as flax, increase the body's metabolic rate, helping to burn the excess, unhealthy fats in the body. Eating the right kind of fat gives your body a better chance to store the right amount of fats. This is called thermogenesis, a process in which specialized fat cells throughout the body (called brown fat) click into high gear and burn more fat when activated by essential fatty acids.

TAKE two tablespoons crushed flax seeds in one of your daily smoothies.

psyllium husks

Psyllium is a natural, water-soluble, gel-reducing fibre that is extracted from the husks of blond psyllium seeds (*Plantago ovata*). The bulking effect of psyllium also works to rid the colon of toxic substances, including heavy metals, as it acts almost as a sponge to soak them off the walls of the intestine. This spongy action has a dual advantage as it can decrease hunger when taken with meals. Since psyllium primarily acts by absorbing water and adding more bulk to the stool, it encourages the normal peristaltic (contracting) action of the bowel. Stimulant laxatives, on the other hand, contain chemicals that cause the intestine to increase the secretion of water. They can often create strong contractions of the colon and, if used in excess, can lead to a loss of normal bowel peristalsis and tone. Psyllium also encourages the growth of healthy, 'friendly' intestinal bacteria such as *Lactobacillus acidophilous* and *Bifidobacteria* that are helpful in regulating bowel movements.

TAKE one teaspoon psyllium husks added to a daily juice or smoothie.

yogurt

Yogurt disables and kills unwanted bacteria. The probiotics in live yogurt inhibit the formation of cancer-causing compounds, they help to detoxify your body by reducing inflammation and encouraging the elimination of intestinal parasites. Yogurt also stimulates the kidneys, thus aiding digestion. If you want a satisfying tasty smoothie, a few tablespoons of natural live yogurt could be that magic ingredient. Avoid sweetened yogurts as the sugar content counteracts any beneficial effect as it is antagonistic to the B vitamins that are made from the bacteria naturally found in yogurt.

fish liver oils

Fish oils (especially cod liver oil) are rich in the EPA and DHA omega-3. These are biologically more potent than the ALA omega-3 in flax seeds. Experimental studies suggest that 3–4 g of ALA per day is equivalent to 0.3 g (300 mg) of EPA per day. EPA and DHA are more rapidly incorporated into plasma and membrane lipids and produce effects more rapidly than does ALA. If you have relatively large reserves of omega-6 linolenic acid in your body fat (the result of a poor diet high in processed and fried food), these tend to slow down the formation of long-chain omega-3 fats like EPA and DHA from ALA.

Incorporating a good-quality fish oil supplement will be beneficial to your diet, as it also provides you with a rare dietary form of vitamin D – essential if you have minimum exposure to natural sunlight. And, considering the concerns over high mercury levels in both sea and freshwater fish, refined fish oil supplements may be considered a safer option for your health.

Do check with your doctor if you are taking immune system suppressants or cholesterol-reducing medication as certain types cannot be mixed with fish oil supplements.

TAKE the recommended daily dose for adults – usually one capsule (depending on the brand).

soya

Soya products contain vitamins and minerals in a natural relationship that is complementary to the human body's needs. They are high in isoflavones, which mimic the action of the female sex hormone ooestrogen (good for menopausal women), reduce insulin levels, decrease arteriosclerosis and lower levels of LDL – bad cholesterol. Soya can help lower the risk of cancer, relieve constipation, regulate blood sugar and is a major source of protein in vegetarian diets. Try incorporating soya milk, yogurt, ice cream and tofu into creamy fruit-based smoothies.

milk thistle

Milk thistle or silymarin, is believed to have protective effects on the liver and improve its function. It is typically used to treat liver cirrhosis, chronic hepatitis (liver inflammation) and gallbladder disorders. It is an antioxidant, assists in liver cell regeneration and is used after exposure to chemical and industrial pollutants or adverse effects from excess alcohol or fat consumption. This herb's liver-strengthening properties make it a good supplement to support a juice diet, especially if you think your liver may be over-taxed and in need of a little extra nurturing.

TAKE the recommended daily dose for adults.

seeds and nuts

Seeds can be thrown into smoothies for super boosts of a whole host of vital nutrients. Flax seeds, sesame, pumpkin and sunflower seeds are rich in protein, A, D, E and B complex vitamins, as well as minerals and unsaturated omega-3 fatty acids. Because of their oil contents they should be kept in the refrigerator or the oils will oxidize, spoiling their taste and nutritional value.

Nuts are a concentrated food source. They are full of protein, vitamins, unsaturated omega-3 fatty acids and minerals, especially selenium and are an effective antioxidant. They reduce levels of bad cholesterol and contain anti-cancer and heart protective qualities. Add freshly ground nuts to smoothies for extra flavour and nutrition.

ginger and garlic

Ginger is a fantastic ingredient, long used by Asians for chest congestion, colds, diarrhoea and nausea. It is naturally antibiotic and anti-inflammatory and boosts HDL – good cholesterol. It has also been attributed with antidepressant powers. It strengthens the immune system and can add anything from gentle warmth to fiery heat, depending on how much you throw into the blend.

Garlic is a member of the onion family and has been called the 'wonder drug'. It is truly one of the world's oldest medicines. Raw garlic is a powerful antibiotic that fights bacteria, parasites and viruses. Two to three cloves a day lessens the chance of heart attacks and strokes, and garlic contains many anti-cancer compounds including allylic sulphides. It boosts immunity, lowers cholesterol and blood pressure. It is at its most powerful when raw, although still potent when cooked. Add a raw clove or two into savoury juices for a real health kick.

brewer's yeast

Brewer's yeast (*Saccharomyces cerevisiae*) is inactive yeast, meaning the yeasts have been killed and have no leavening power. It is the yeast remaining after beer-making and is used as a nutrient supplement to increase the intake of B vitamins. Brewer's yeast is rich in many basic nutrients such as B vitamins, amino acids and at least 14 different minerals. The protein content of yeast is responsible for 52 per cent of its weight. Because of its B vitamin content it is a great physical and mental energy boost between meals. It helps metabolism, is good for eczema, heart disorders, gout, nervousness and fatigue. Brewer's yeast comes powdered (the most potent form), in flakes and in tablets. It can be added to drinks, sprinkled over food or eaten alone. Make sure you use brewer's yeast and not active baker's yeast as they are totally different in their functions.

Because of its high phosphorus content it is not recommended for people suffering with osteoporosis. If you are taking large amounts of yeast you should make sure to get adequate calcium in the diet. Supplementation of one tablespoon of brewer's yeast a day should be enough. Also avoid brewer's yeast if you have a chronic yeast problem (systemic candidiasis).

TAKE the recommended daily dose for adults, depending on the brand.

BUYING SUPPLEMENTS

When buying supplements such as milk thistle and brewer's yeast, buy as good quality as you can afford. Bulk buying may seem like a good idea but it can be a false economy because the ingredients may be inferior and lessen the effectiveness of the supplement over time. For maximum freshness, keep all supplements refrigerated in their jars.

is this the diet for you?

Before you start any diet you should determine whether it is **appropriate** for you. Consider the various issues raised below before you embark on any **diet plan**.

weighty matters

Are you overweight? If so, how overweight? According to the World Health Organization (WHO), there are more than 1 billion overweight adults globally, at least 300 million of whom are obese. But what is obese? It is easy to over-dramatize your weight predicament and take measures that are overly extreme and unnecessary. Obesity and overweight are words that are often used interchangeably, so let's clarify the difference between obese and overweight. Overweight refers to an excess of body weight, which includes all tissues, such as fat, bone and muscle but not necessarily body fat. Obesity means that a person is carrying an excessively high proportion of body fat that could compromise their health.

If you are an athlete or body-builder, the chances are you may weigh in at over the desirable weight range for your height (see below) but this is normal as muscle weighs more than fat. You could be a relatively sedentary person who weighs in at the correct weight for your height, but who still carries too high a proportion of body fat for your size. In which case, a good exercise programme is vital.

Body Mass Index (BMI)

The easiest way to determine how severe your weight problem is, apart from simply looking in the mirror or trying to do up your 'skinny jeans', is to work out your Body Mass Index (BMI). The BMI is the common method of evaluating individual people to see if they are under- or overweight. It involves comparing their weight to their height by dividing the weight (in kg) by the square of their height (in metres). Work out your BMI by using the chart opposite. A BMI of below 18.5 is underweight, between

RISK OF ASSOCIATED DISEASE ACCORDING TO BMI AND WAIST SIZE

	BMI 18.5 or less (Underweight)	BMI 18.5–24.9 (Normal)	BMI 25.0–29.9 (Overweight)	BMI 30.0–34.9 (Obese)	BMI 35.0–39.9 (Morbidly obese)	BMI 40 or greater (Extremely obese)
Waist less than or equal to 94 cm (37 in) men; 80 cm (32 in) women	N/A	N/A	Increased	High risk	Very high risk	Extremely high risk
Waist greater than 94 cm (37 in) men; 80 cm (32 in) women	N/A	N/A	High	Very high risk	Very high risk	Extremely high risk

18.5 and 25 is an indication of healthy weight, 25 to 30 is overweight, a BMI of over 30 is referred to as obese, over 35 is known as morbid obesity and over 40 indicates extreme obesity.

Now you need to get the tape measure out as a recent report by the WHO suggests that increased risk of chronic and dehabilitating disease is present when the waist measurement of men exceeds 94 cm (37 in) and for women 80 cm (32 in). So where do you stand? If your BMI is higher than 30, please check with your doctor before embarking on this programme.

detox issues

Even though weight loss may be the primary objective and motivation for you choosing this diet, you may need it more than you realize. You might be one of the many people who has learned to live in the 'discomfort' zone as a result of a toxic overload from the daily assault of pesticides, additives, antibiotics, hormones, preservatives and environmental pollutants. Your body may be showing signs of distress and sending you clear messages that all is not well.

Persistent health problems such as skin disorders, hormonal imbalances, headaches, fatigue, disturbed sleep patterns and inexplicable pains, particularly under the right shoulder blade can indicate a toxic liver.

All is probably not well with your colon if you have excessive gas, constipation or diarrhoea, lower back pain, abdominal discomfort, multiple food allergies or bad breath.

If you are suffering from a toxic liver or impaired elimination due to a sluggish and toxic colon, along with frequent colds, runny nose, sinus problems, lethargy, mental exhaustion and premature ageing, what you categorically don't have is vibrant health.

check with your doctor

Before you start the diet, it is important to stress that, just like any other dietary programme there are groups of people for whom this diet isn't suitable. If any of the following applies to you, then this may not be your ideal weight-loss regime. In fact, you should check with a qualified medical practitioner before embarking on any new dietary programme.

* Pregnant or lactating women
* Diabetics
* Hypoglycemia
* Wilson's disease
* IBS
* Degenerative AIDS
* Pre-surgery or post-surgery patients
* If you are over 65 or under 18

getting physical

10 great exercise ideas

The human body is designed for movement, not slouching in front of the television or bent over a computer. **Moving** your body is essential if you want to **shift** the pounds and **stay fit**.

You should aim to exercise for a minimum of 30 minutes a day. But if the idea of trundling along to your local gym and hitting the machines fills you with dread, or the mere mention of the words 'aerobics class' brings you out in a rash, fear not – there are many alternative forms of exercise that may suit you better.

1 belly dancing is brilliant for tightening the muscles of the stomach, waist and hips and even your thighs. Plus it is amazing for improving posture and relieving back pain, and also perfect for both ante- and postnatal exercise classes.
Burn around 400 kcals an hour.

2 cycling is something they say you never forget how to do, so why not get on your bike and benefit from a fantastic way to exercise? You can take in some beautiful scenery and get fitter.
Burn a whopping 600 kcals an hour.

3 dancing, whether gentle ballroom or jigging around your lounge to a few of your favourite tunes, is a fabulous way to say goodbye to those excess pounds.
Burn between 400 to 700 kcals an hour.

4 power walking is one of the easiest ways to be physically active. You can do it almost anywhere and at any time. Power walking is also inexpensive; all you need is a pair of shoes with sturdy heel support. It is the perfect way to get a bit of cardiovascular exercise, not only while on this diet but every day as it allows for many levels of fitness.
Burn 300 kcals in a good one-hour walk.

5 gardening, if you have green fingers and a garden to look after, is an enjoyable way to combine a creative hobby and physical activity, but you do need to get down to the more intensive jobs such as weeding and lawn-mowing to really burn off those excess pounds.
Burn around 300 kcals per hour.

6 jogging is cheap, you can do it almost anywhere, and it is a great way to take a little time out and disappear into your own thoughts. It also gets you out and about in the fresh air. Make sure you invest in a decent pair of running shoes to minimize any damaging impact.
Burn around 300 kcals on a 30-minute jog.

7 martial arts are spiritually, mentally and physically uplifting exercise experiences that tone every part of your body. If you are the sort of person who can focus and absorb yourself totally in an activity, you will find this very relaxing and invigorating.
Burn up to 400 kcals per hour.

8 skipping will burn serious calories and involves minimal investment – a rope that is long enough to turn easily. Then all you need is sufficient space to twirl your rope. Wear comfortable training shoes with a good sole.
Burn around 300 kcals if you skip for 30 minutes.

9 swimming is a great all-round, no-impact way to exercise your whole body. The more you put in to it, the more you will lose in calorie-burning terms. Wear good-quality goggles to ensure you keep going for longer.
Burn between 200 and 300 kcals for a 30-minute swim.

10 pilates is a low-impact exercise regime that focuses on strengthening your core – a flat tummy being the added bonus. It is vital to take lessons initially as each exercise must be done properly, in the correct position, to ensure maximum results. For overall fitness combine Pilates with a cardiovascular form of exercise such as jogging.

Burn around 300 kcals per hour.

gentle daily workout

Although training for the marathon or any other form of strenuous exercise isn't a great idea while you are on this diet, you should indulge in regular **physical activity** in order to maximize weight loss. By combining the exercises on the following pages with **30 minutes** of walking each day you will be well on your way to a healthier, leaner body. As with any exercise programme it is essential that you **warm up** and **cool down** properly.

Warm-up and cool down

SIDE REACHES

KNEE PULL

Reach one arm over your head and to the side. Keep your hips steady and your shoulders straight to the side. Hold for 10 seconds and repeat on the other side.

Stand up straight keeping your head, hips and feet in a straight line. Pull one knee to your chest, hold for 10 seconds, then repeat with the other leg.

CALF STRETCH

Step forward with one leg and bend your knee. Keep the back leg straight and the foot flat on the floor. Hold for 10 seconds, then repeat with the other leg.

TRICEP STRETCH

Cross one arm over your chest and pull the elbow closer to your body using the other hand. Hold for 10 seconds and repeat on the other side.

THIGH STRETCH

Pull your left foot to your buttocks with your left hand (or both hands). Keep your knee pointing straight to the ground. Hold for 10 seconds. Repeat with your right foot.

PECTORAL STRETCH

Keeping chest out and chin in, lift your arms behind you until you feel stretch in arms, shoulder and chest. Hold for 10 seconds.

Upper body
ARM CIRCLES

1 Stand up straight with your feet hip-width apart and your arms outstretched to the sides at shoulder height. Move the wrists and palms of your hands in small clockwise circles for the count of 10.

2 Now repeat the movement, anti-clockwise, while you count to 10. Repeat the exercise 4 times.

CHEST PRESS

1 Stand up straight, feet hip-width apart. Lift your arms to shoulder height and bend at your elbows.

2 Bring your arms together in front of your body so your forearms press against each other. Return to starting position and repeat 10 times.

BICEP CURL

1 Stand up straight with your arms by your sides and fists clenched.

2 Curl your arms towards your shoulders focusing on the bicep muscles. Lower your arms back to your sides and repeat 10 times.

GENTLE PUSH-UPS

1 Start by kneeling on all fours, with your hands flat on the floor, slightly more than shoulder-width apart.

2 Bend your arms and gently lower yourself down. Return to the starting position and repeat 10 times.

Legs, Tums and Bums
WIDE SQUATS

1 Begin by standing with your legs wide apart and hands on your hips.

2 Bend your knees until they are just over your toes, keeping your back straight. Return to the starting position and repeat 10 times.

CALF RAISES

1 Stand up straight with your legs together, your hands on your hips and your feet flat on the floor.

2 Raise your heels and lift yourself up on to your toes, hold for 1 second then lower. Repeat 10 times.

UPPER LEG RAISES

1 Lie on your side with one leg on top of the other and your hips facing forwards. Support your head with your forearm.

2 Slowly raise the top leg, then lower it back down. Repeat 10 times on this leg, then 10 times on the other leg.

LOWER LEG RAISES

1 Take up the same starting position as above, then bend the top leg over the bottom leg and rest on the floor, keeping your hips central.

2 Slowly lift the lower leg until it's in line with your body. Hold for 1 second, then lower it. Repeat 10 times on this leg, then 10 times on the other leg.

Abs and back
GENTLE SIT-UPS

1 Lie on your back with your knees bent and your arms behind your head to support its weight. Contract your tummy muscles as if trying to push your navel against your spine.

2 Lift your head and shoulders, hold for 1 second, then lower. Repeat 10 times.

SIDE CURLS

1 Lie on your back with your knees bent at a right angle, your ankles either touching or crossed and your arms behind your head to support its weight.

2 Lift your head and shoulders and, twisting from your waist, raise your right elbow towards your left knee. Repeat 5 times with the right elbow and 5 times with the left.

BACK RAISES

1 Lie on your front with your elbows bent and your hands on the back of your head.

2 Contract your tummy muscles and slowly lift your head, neck and shoulders off the floor. Lower slowly back down and repeat 10 times.

SIDE-TO-SIDE

1 Lie on your back, lift your legs and bend your knees so that your shins are parallel to the floor. Stretch your arms out to the sides in line with your shoulders.

2 Contract your tummy muscles and move both your knees to one side and lower them towards the floor, keeping your shoulders still. Return your legs to the starting position and repeat 5 times on the left side and then 5 times on the right.

gentle daily workout   **41**

pre-diet plan

getting started

Although it might be very tempting to jump straight in and get juicing, please bear in mind that some **preparation** is needed especially if you smoke, drink caffeine and alcohol, eat junk food and take medicine at the first sign of discomfort.

Stripping these things from your diet can cause withdrawal symptoms that may cause you difficulty. But with the correct preparation, this can be minimized.

In order to promote weight loss, this diet will have a detoxifying effect on your body. This will renew and refresh you, but can cause various side effects as your body rids itself of the toxins that have been keeping you bloated and overweight. As the toxins work their way out from your tissues into the bloodstream you could experience some of the following common detox symptoms: spots and rashes, headaches, body odour, bad breath, nausea, runny nose, diarrhoea or constipation, flu-like symptoms, slight depression or mood swings. Reactions will differ greatly from person to person as not everyone is affected equally due to differences in body chemistry. How well we metabolize (break down and get rid of) foreign chemicals depends on our genetic ability and on the extent of the environmental burden of chemicals challenging us.

Even though you may think that you have a healthy diet, toxins aren't just produced by food and drink. Your body will rid itself of any unwanted chemicals, including the chemicals from your own metabolism or that enter your system from the air you breathe, the food and water you consume, substances you put on to your skin or use to treat your hair, or toxins and allergens produced by the germs that inhabit your intestine. But, a few days preparation can minimize any negative side effects, making it easier for you to stick to the plan and maximize your weight loss.

CUT IT OUT!

For a week before starting the diet, cut out the following:

* Coffee and tea
* Alcohol
* White bread and bread products
* White rice
* Refined sugar
* Salt
* Fizzy drinks
* Bottled cordials and juice 'drinks'
* Sweets
* Chocolate
* Margarine
* Sweet biscuits and cakes
* Crisps and salted nuts
* Canned fruit and vegetables
* Processed meat products such as burgers and sausages
* Sugary cereals
* Sweet fruit low-fat yogurts
* Ice cream and ice-lollies
* White pasta
* Pre-packaged convenience meals
* Sauces and gravy mixes
* Take-away foods such as pizza and Chinese

the baddies

Here are the five big dietary baddies or as I like to call them 'the **enemies** of your weight and more importantly, your health'. Here's why you need to **cut them out** of your diet.

1 caffeine I know you are probably reeling in shock – how can you do without your *grande latte*, but sorry, this just has to go. It has a very dehydrating effect on your system; a disaster if you also don't drink enough water.

You can feel the effects of caffeine in your system within a few minutes of ingesting it and it stays in your system for four to six hours. While in your body, caffeine affects the following hormones:

* **Adenosine** Caffeine inhibits absorption of adenosine, which calms the body; although caffeine can make you feel alert in the short run, it can cause sleep problems later.
* **Adrenaline** Caffeine injects adrenaline into your system, giving you a temporary boost, but possibly making you fatigued and depressed later. If you take more caffeine to counteract these effects, you end up spending the day in an agitated state and might find yourself jumpy and edgy by night.
* **Cortisol** Caffeine increase the body's levels of cortisol, the 'stress hormone', which can lead to other health consequences ranging from weight gain and moodiness to heart disease and diabetes.
* **Dopamine** Caffeine increases dopamine levels in your system, acting in a similar way to amphetamines, which can make you feel good after taking it, but after it wears off you can feel 'low'. It can also lead to a physical dependence because of dopamine manipulation.

These changes that caffeine makes in your physiology can have negative consequences on your sleep patterns and even your weight. Many experts believe that increased levels of cortisol lead to stronger cravings for fats and carbohydrates, and cause the body to store fat in the abdomen. (Abdominal fat carries with it greater health risks than other types of fat.)

It is highly addictive and if you normally consume a lot of coffee, tea, fizzy drinks or even chocolate – another not so obvious source – then you will definitely suffer if you don't reduce your regular caffeine intake gradually.

Initially reduce your intake by half, replacing it with a cup of caffeine-free Rooibos tea, herbal infusions or even hot water and lemon. Then after a couple of days reduce it by half again and then two or three days before you are due to begin the Miracle Juice Diet, eradicate it completely. You will gradually feel your energy rise as your diet improves and your sleep patterns normalize.

2 refined carbohydrates In the US over 70 per cent of the population eats a diet that is high in refined carbohydrates. This is a disaster, since stripping out the fibre and nutrients from flour and sugar in order to make them look appealingly white, we are making them nutritionally empty.

Food processing removes magnesium, zinc and chromium from flour and sugar, the three minerals the body needs to metabolize carbohydrates properly. It also drastically reduces vitamins B1, B2, B3, calcium and iron. So avoid junk foods that are made up of refined flour and sugar, and their equally bad counterparts – processed fats, colourings, flavourings and preservatives.

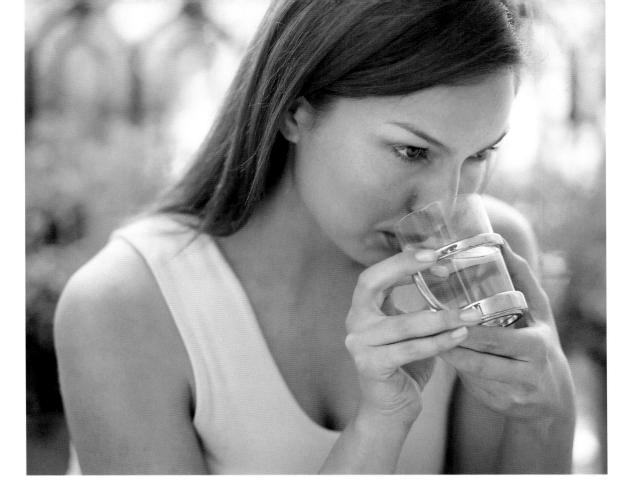

3 **alcohol** Alcohol is probably the most widely abused drug on the planet. Worryingly, the chronic, progressive and potentially fatal disease alcoholism affects one out of ten people in the Western world. The biggest strain is felt by the liver, which works very hard to neutralize the effects of drinking on the body by breaking down the composition of the alcohol. There are many nutrients that can help the liver detoxify alcohol, but unfortunately their action is impaired by the alcohol itself, which can interfere with their stores in the body, or prevent the absorption of vital enzymes in the liver that activate these nutrients. For example, the liver will expel all of its folic acid into the bloodstream when alcohol is consumed. This will cause a deficiency that has a knock-on effect. Folic acid is needed to work with vitamin B12 to stimulate the formation of red blood cells. Reduce the levels of one of those nutrients and the whole cycle is compromised. Ever wondered why you look so pale with a hangover?

4 **hydrogenated fats** Hydrogenation is one of the processes that can be used to turn liquid oil into solid fat. The final product of this process is called hydrogenated fat. It is used in some biscuits, cakes, pastry, margarines and other processed foods.

During the process of hydrogenation, trans fats may be formed. These are harmful and have no known nutritional benefits. They raise LDL (bad) cholesterol in the blood, which increases the risk of coronary heart disease, and lower HDL (good) cholesterol. Some evidence suggests that the effects of trans fats may be worse than saturated fats.

5 **salt** Although it's been a flavour enhancer and preservative through much of human history, the health effects of salt have aroused suspicion as long ago as ancient China when excess salt consumption was believed to increase pulse rate. Today, numerous studies have linked high salt intake to a rise in blood pressure. In some people, this could lead to hypertension – pressure higher than 140/90mm Hg, which raises the risk of stroke, heart attack and kidney damage.

what to eat

Plenty! Of the right stuff, that is. First and foremost are those great
friends of health, fruit and vegetables, unrefined carbs
and good proteins along with healthy fats and plenty of water.

fruit and veg

Allow yourself loads of slow-release carbohydrates — fresh, organic fruit, vegetables and juices in the week leading to the Miracle Juice Diet. Organic fruits and vegetables contain more vitamins and trace elements and are free from chemical fertilizers and insecticides. Maybe try out a few of the juice recipes.

carbs

Instead of piling up your plate with fries or pasta, opt for healthy brown rice or a sweet potato in its jacket. Have rye bread instead of white or a few healthy oatcakes. Experiment with new grains like quinoa or millet.

protein

Boost your body's stores of fat-soluble vitamins by having good-quality protein twice a day. Choose from:

* Fish and shellfish: trout, sardines, mackerel, fresh tuna, cod, bass, sole, herring, tinned tuna, dory, haddock, halibut, snapper, swordfish, green-lipped mussels, squid, oysters, clams, crayfish, lobster, crab, scallops, prawns, all rich in omega-3 fatty acids.
* Poultry and game: organic or free-range chicken, turkey, wild duck, pheasant, quail, rabbit, venison, wild boar.
* Free-range, organic eggs.
* Soya: tofu, tempeh, edamame beans, soya milk and yogurt.

healthy fats

You will need to have some healthy unsaturated fats as they contain two fatty acids that are essential to life, and that the body cannot produce itself. They are linoleic acid (omega-6) and linolenic acid (omega-3). Out of these two essential fatty acids your body can make all the other fatty acids it needs. So, do include some healthy fat in your diet and build up your reserves of the fat-soluble vitamins.

Include a little of the following as they are great sources of the right kind of fats:

* Flax seed oil and flax seeds, hemp oil and hemp seeds, tofu, olive oil, walnuts, sunflower seeds, pumpkin seeds, almonds, avocado, macadamia nuts, olives, tahini.

Even though coconut oil is classed as a saturated fat, it is meant to have health-boosting properties – just don't

PRE-DIET DIET
Your daily diet should look something like this:
BREAKFAST: Porridge with fresh fruit and a dollop of natural live yogurt OR two poached eggs on rye toast
SNACK: 25 g (1 oz) sunflower seeds OR one of the juices from the book
LUNCH: Chicken and salad sandwich on rye bread OR tuna salad and an apple
SNACK: A pear OR 25 g (1 oz) Brazil nuts
DINNER: Salmon steak with stir-fried mixed vegetables and brown rice OR turkey breast with steamed vegetables and a small sweet potato
And remember to reduce your caffeine intake.

over-use it. Plus, oily fish is also full of omega 3 fatty acids, so don't forget to have at least two to three portions per week.

water

Drink water, which is essential to start flushing those toxins from your body and keep your system hydrated. Did you know that sometimes when you think that you feel hungry, you are actually thirsty? So try to drink at least eight glasses of water per day.

the basic rules again

So now you should have a pretty clear idea of what you will have to do, but just to reiterate, here is a basic outline of the rules.

* Prepare for the seven-day juice regime by cutting out all caffeine, alcohol and junk food for at least a week before.
* During this week eat the majority of your fruit and vegetables raw to ensure a good level of phytonutrients and fibre.
* Increase your intake of healthy omega-3 fatty acids by eating more oily fish and only using natural unrefined oils in your cooking.

* Eat more high-quality protein, organic if possible.
* Drink at least eight glasses of water per day.
* Incorporate 20–40 minutes of aerobic exercise into your daily routine and do the 15-minute gentle stretching and toning session once a day.

so, are you all fired up?

You should be. You are giving your body a rest from all the bad things you have been eating, and will be cleansing and nourishing your system. This will help you view food more as vital fuel that allows your body to function at its optimum level. This may be your turning point. You may actually change your attitude from one of 'Oh no, I'm on a diet,' to a more positive 'I am doing this for me, to make myself healthier, fitter, stronger, leaner.'

Get excited; pretty soon you are going to be feeling and looking loads better. Think of that boost of self-confidence you are going to experience. All those clothes that have been lurking at the back of your wardrobe, like your skinny jeans, will fit again. So get ready, whatever weight you have to lose, this is only going to work if you are committed to changing your eating and exercise habits for life.

motivational tips

It never ceases to amaze me that people will lavish care and attention on their homes and cars, keep totally up-to-date with the latest high-tech gizmos and gadgets, throw unlimited time and attention into their work, and yet **treat their bodies** with little or **no regard**.

You can buy a new house, cars can be replaced and you can get yourself a new job, but these things will fade into unimportance if your body starts to let you down. So, maybe it's time to get serious about your health and get yourself into better shape. Don't view the diet as a period of denial; use it as an opportunity to get fitter and feel better.

the power of five per cent

If you are overweight, losing as little as five per cent of your body weight may lower your risk of developing the major health problems listed below.

* Type 2 diabetes
* Heart disease and stroke
* Cancer
* Sleep apnea
* Osteoarthritis
* Gallbladder disease
* Fatty liver disease

A diet high in sugar can raise insulin levels and develop into diabetes. Over 18 million people suffer from Type 2 diabetes in the UK alone. This condition can lead to blindness and even amputations. Additives can stimulate the production of hormones that can encourage the growth of certain cancer cells. Junk food also contains unhealthy fats that can raise cholesterol levels and lead to heart disease. According to the World Health Organization, over 85 per cent of major diseases are caused by what we put into our mouths.

germ warfare

Your immune system is designed to defend you against millions of bacteria, microbes, viruses, toxins and parasites that are continually trying to invade your body. This diet will help keep you well on a daily basis as all the juices and smoothies are bursting with immune-boosting nutrients such as vitamins A and C. Plus, they also contain all the minerals and phytonutrients necessary to enable successful absorption and utilization of these vitamins. As a result you won't be so prone to minor ailments such as colds and flu, and you will be strengthening your resistance to more serious conditions.

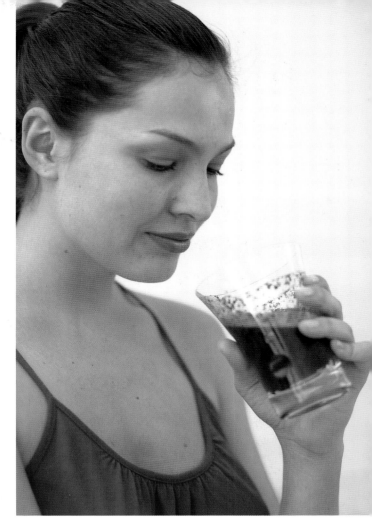

put the spring back in your step

Caffeine is the most widely used drug in the world and it's no coincidence that its use has increased alongside longer working hours. Along with regular sugar consumption, it is the stimulant of choice for many people who would vehemently deny that they had any form of addiction. Yet both those substances play havoc with energy levels and cause mood swings and fatigue. Throw alcohol into the equation and you will have a body that is suffering from extreme stress – from a health perspective this a time bomb waiting to explode.

Even though you may find this hard to believe, your energy levels will soar after a few days on the diet, especially if you have been diligent about following the advised preparation plan (pages 44–9) and minimized the withdrawal symptoms. You will be more productive, sleep better and feel refreshed.

how to juice

If you are going to incorporate healthy juices and smoothies into your life, the first step is to get yourself **equipped** with the proper appliances.

My best advice is to spend as much as you can afford on reputable brand-name, good-quality machines. Cheaper ones may seem a bargain but they seem not to be able to stand regular use, and often the cheaper the juicer, the lower quality the juice. Shop around, look online for special offers, but get the best machines you can afford.

HELPFUL JUICING HINTS

* Use fresh, firm fruits and vegetables for maximum nutrient content.
* Wash all fruits and vegetables thoroughly to remove any dirt or chemicals.
* Remove all stems and large stones.
* Do not force fruits and vegetables through the juicer. Pass through slowly and steadily using the pusher provided – never use knives or other metal kitchen implements.
* Do not cut fruits and vegetables too small – cut to a size that fits comfortably into the chute.
* Alternate soft fruits and harder fruits and vegetables; this will help push the softer fruits through.
* When juicing leafy vegetables, roll into a ball and push through followed by harder fruit or vegetables.
* Don't try to juice bananas, avocados or very over-ripe fruit – this will clog up the juicer. Use these in smoothies.
* Never juice rhubarb, aubergine, coconut or leeks.

You may already have a citrus press, which is fine for extracting juice from citrus fruit, but in all honesty, it is better to use a proper juicer as you will benefit from the nutrients held in the pith and pips.

blender

Look for a sturdy, well-made blender that has a variety of speeds as you will need to be able to crush ice and blend frozen fruit. Hand-held immersion blenders are not really designed to do this and could be very messy unless you have a very deep container. The liquid will fly everywhere.

juicers

There are two main types of juicer – centrifugal and masticating – and whatever you choose, the key point to note is that the drier the pulp, the more effective the juicer.

* **Centrifugal** This is the most widely used and affordable juicer. The fruits and vegetables are fed into a rapidly spinning grater, the juice and pulp is separated, and a smaller amount of juice is produced than by a masticating or pulverizing juicer.
* **Masticating** The larger, more expensive juicers operate by masticating or pulverizing the fruit and vegetables. These are pushed through a wire mesh; the action is very powerful and produces a high level of juice with very dry pulp. The juice is more nutrient-dense as not only is there more of it, the juice hasn't been extracted via a spinning metal blade that produces heat, which in turn kills those vital enzymes.

cleaning chores

The most aggravating aspect of juicing is cleaning the machine – it has to be done as soon as you have finished juicing, and it has to be thorough, as any residue will encourage bacterial growth. So look out for a machine that dismantles easily.

Most machines come with a special brush to clean the mesh or grater. I have found wire-cleaning pads excellent for the job. Soaking in warm soapy water can also make the task a little easier. If the plastic parts of the machine become stained, use a mixture of one part white vinegar to two parts water to remove the discolouration.

monitoring weight loss

There are definitely two schools of thought on how to do this – either you go for the daily **weighing** or the once a week weigh-in.

This is an entirely individual issue. If you are the sort of person who needs that daily date with your weighing scales, then by all means do it. If you prefer the 'surprise at the end of the week' approach, then this is fine, too. But whatever your preferred method of keeping track of your progress, you should have a tight-fitting pair of trousers or other item of clothing that is a little too close for comfort, and try it on at the beginning and end of the seven days. On a more long-term basis, if you are exercising regularly and increasing your muscle-to-fat ratio, you may even end up weighing slightly more, as muscle tissue is heavier, but your shape will be trimmer.

dietary demons

One of the most difficult things to deal with when you are trying to stick to a diet is the friend or relative who tries to lure you off course. You know the ones; they usually arrive with a little treat and try to persuade you that one little deviation won't matter. It will. Don't be bullied into breaking your resolve. Politely decline and say that you are relying on them for support. If you are visiting, take a juice or smoothie with you. Even better, if those friends could do with losing a few pounds, try and get them to join you.

snack attacks

Even though you should feel satisfied on this diet, you could undermine your efforts very easily by hitting the biscuit jar in a moment of weakness. It really is better to clear out anything vaguely tempting from the refrigerator and cupboards. If you have a family and this isn't possible, then you are going to have to be very careful, particularly at times that you normally seek a bit of comfort food.

One woman who couldn't stop herself snacking on her kids' leftovers used to douse the plates in washing-up liquid the minute the kids left the table. A bit extreme, but unless you like cold fries and chicken nuggets with a side order of soap, it might prove a very effective way of keeping temptation at bay.

shopping list

Careful planning is essential when embarking on this diet to ensure you have all of the **ingredients necessary** to prepare the juices and won't be tempted to cheat.

If you have a large enough refrigerator and freezer, one big shop will be sufficient, but if your space is limited then you may find you need to shop twice – which is good from the freshness perspective. As mentioned earlier, freezing juices works very well, but it may not be practical to make all 35 drinks at one time. It might be more practical for you to make the majority of your juices and smoothies the night before.

FROM THE HEALTH FOOD STORE

Dried apricots

Brewer's yeast – B-complex

Flax seeds

Milk thistle/silymarin tablets

Probiotics

Psyllium husks

Sunflower seeds/pumpkin seeds

Variety of unsalted nuts

FROM THE CHILLER CABINET

Cranberry juice

Natural live yogurt

Tomato juice

FRESH HERBS

Basil

Fresh chillies

Coriander

Mint

FRUITS

Apples

Avocado

Banana

Blackberries – frozen or fresh

Blueberries – frozen or fresh

Cherries

Clementines

Grapefruit

Grapes

Kiwifruit

Lemons

Limes

Melon

Mango

Oranges

Papaya

Passion fruit

Pears

Pineapple

Plums

Raspberries – frozen or fresh

Strawberries

VEGETABLES

Beetroot

Broccoli

Carrots

Celery

Cucumber

Fennel

Fresh root ginger

Onion

Peppers – red/green/yellow/orange

Red cabbage

Spinach

Spring onions

Sweet potato

Tomatoes

Watercress

DRIED HERBS AND SPICES

Camomile

Cloves

Dandelion

Fennel seeds

Star anise

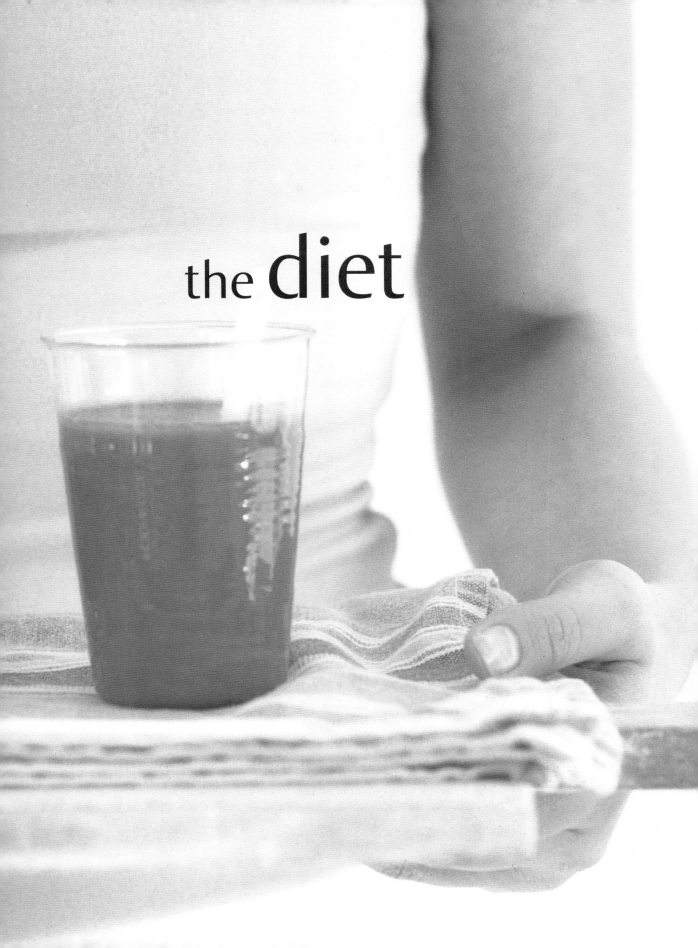

the diet

day 1

This is the first day and with all your **preparations** in place, you should be **raring** to go

OK, day one is here. Let your juicer and blender take pole position in the kitchen. If you have followed the advice for the preparation week, you should be totally in the zone and already feeling a little lighter and a lot healthier. Good luck.

◄ flat belly berry

Apples are excellent for cleansing the system and, along with blueberries and cranberries, they are packed full of vitamins C and E, and minerals calcium, magnesium and phosphorus.

3 apples
150 ml (5 fl oz) unsweetened cranberry juice
125 g (4 oz) fresh or frozen blueberries
1 tablespoon powdered psyllium husks

Juice the apples, and then whizz the apple juice in a blender with the cranberry juice, blueberries and powdered psyllium husks.

Makes 300 ml (10 fl oz) or 1 large glass
Vitamin C 70 mg • Magnesium 25 mg • Calories 270

on today's menu

start the day
Lemon and Ginger Infusion (page 62)

and then on to
Flat Belly Berry (page 59)
Spicy Pear (page 60)
Lean Green (page 60)
Chilli Orange (page 62)
Big Red (page 62)

and wind down with
Any herbal tea or infusion of your choice
2 teaspoons flax seeds

snack attack
25 g (1 oz) sunflower seeds plus 1 apple

spicy pear ▶

Pears are a gentle laxative, while celery acts as a diuretic and root ginger promotes good digestion, making this a great juice for keeping your system balanced.

150 g (5 oz) pear
75 g (3 oz) celery
2.5 cm (1 inch) piece of fresh root ginger

Juice all the ingredients together and either serve over ice or whizz in a blender with a couple of ice cubes for a smoother, creamier drink.

Makes 300 ml (10 fl oz) or 1 large glass
Vitamin C 30 mg • Calcium 110 mg • Calories 75

lean green

Refreshing, green and healthy, this sweet and savoury juice is bursting with goodness.

200 g (7 oz) pineapple
100 g (3½ oz) broccoli
100 g (3½ oz) cucumber
1 kiwifruit

Juice the pineapple and broccoli, then blend with the cucumber and kiwifruit along with a couple of ice cubes.

Makes 300 ml (10 fl oz) or 1 large glass
Vitamin C 160 mg • Calcium 128 mg • Iron 2.7 mg
• Calories 161

TOP TIP

Instead of drinking your juices and smoothies quickly, take time to actually taste and enjoy the flavours. Allow the juice to rest in your mouth for a while, since this will stimulate the production of the salivary digestive enzyme amylase.

chilli orange

This juice is full of vitamin C and the enzymes in the pineapple are great at dissolving the mucus that can accumulate in your system if you have a build-up of toxins. The chillies not only give this juice a bit of a kick, they are rich in carotenoids.

250 g (8 oz) carrot
250 g (8 oz) pineapple
$1/2$ lime, peeled
$1/2$ small chilli, deseeded
1 tablespoon chopped coriander leaves

Juice the carrot, pineapple and lime, then throw into a blender with the chillies, coriander and a couple of ice cubes.

Makes 200 ml (7 fl oz) or 1 small glass
Vitamin C 72 mg • Selenium 4 mcg • Calories 240

big red

This juice is full of phytonutrients including lycopene, which has been proven to have anti-cancer properties.

200 g (7 oz) hulled strawberries
400 g (14 oz) tomatoes
a few basil leaves

Juice all the ingredients together and serve over ice cubes.

Makes 400 ml (14 fl oz) or 1 very large glass
Vitamin C 222 mg • Calcium 60 mg • Magnesium 48 mg • Calories 122

LITTLE HOTTY
LEMON AND GINGER INFUSION
Chop up half a lemon and a cube of fresh root ginger, place in a cafetiere or teapot and top up with hot water. Let it infuse for about three minutes then drink. You can have as many of these as you want during the day.

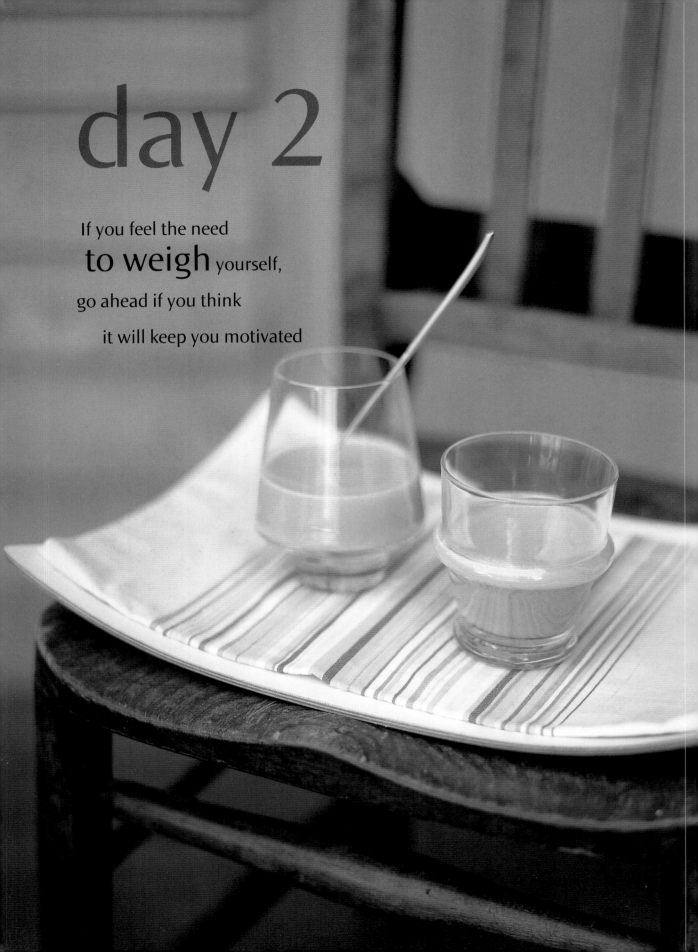

day 2

If you feel the need
to weigh yourself,
go ahead if you think
it will keep you motivated

How are you feeling today? Probably a lot better than you thought you might. Get ready for your first smoothie of the day, which is really delicious and very satisfying. You will notice that you feel less bloated than usual because your body will already be expelling excess fluids from your tissues.

◄ orange super smoothie

This nourishing smoothie is rich in iron, calcium and potassium and high in beta-carotene. Add a handful of sunflower seeds to rev up the omega-3 levels. It will appeal to all the family, especially children, so maybe make extra as a perfect breakfast drink.

1 large carrot
1 orange
100 g (3¹/₂ oz) banana
1 fresh or dried apricot
variation: swop banana for ¹/₂ small avocado

Juice the carrot and orange. Whizz the juice in a blender with the banana (or avocado, if that's what you're using), apricot and a couple of ice cubes.

Makes 200 ml (7 fl oz) or 1 small glass
Vitamin A 44,570 iu • Vitamin C 101 mg
• Potassium 1,475 mg • Iron 2.5 mg • Calories 204

on today's menu

start the day
Fennel Infusion (page 69)

and then on to
Orange Super Smoothie (page 65)
Time Bomb (page 66)
Ruby Smoothie (page 66)
Spicy Lemonade (page 69)
Invigor8 (page 69)

and wind down with
Any herbal tea or infusion of your choice
2 teaspoons flax seeds

snack attack
25 g (1 oz) pumpkin seeds plus 1 pear

ruby smoothie

This highly nutritious and very satisfying smoothie is high in vitamin C, and the combination of the pectin in the apple and probiotics in the yogurt makes it a great choice for the digestive tract.

2 oranges
1 apple
75 g (3 oz) raspberries, fresh or frozen
75 g (3 oz) strawberries, fresh or frozen
150 ml (5 fl oz) natural live yogurt

Juice the oranges and apple, then whizz the juice in a blender with the raspberries, strawberries and yogurt. Serve immediately.

Makes 400 ml (14 fl oz) or 1 very large glass
Vitamin C 145 mg • Vitamin E 1.81 mg • Calcium 407 mg
• Iron 2 mg • Zinc 1.65 mg • Calories 283

time bomb ▶

All three ingredients in this bright green juice are high in magnesium and vitamin C, which is essential for healthy functioning of the adrenal glands and the liver. If you are going through a prolonged period of stress, your body may be lacking these two vital nutrients as they are easily depleted when the going gets tough.

150 g (5 oz) spinach
150 g (5 oz) broccoli
2 medium tomatoes

Wash all three ingredients and juice. Serve in a tumbler with a stick of celery if liked.

Makes 200 ml (7 fl oz) or 1 small glass
Vitamin A 14,234 iu • Vitamin C 202 mg
• Magnesium 171 mg • Calories 120

spicy lemonade

This is great diluted with a little hot (not boiling) water and served as a warm drink. A little cinnamon sprinkled over the top tastes great, and if you like your drinks quite sour, add an extra squeeze of lemon.

3 apples
$^1/_2$ lemon, peeled
1 yellow pepper, deseeded
2.5 cm (1 inch) cube fresh root ginger

Juice all the ingredients together and serve over ice cubes.

Makes 250 ml (8 fl oz) or 1 small glass
Vitamin C 190 mg • Calcium 37 mg • Magnesium 52 mg
• Calories 247

LITTLE HOTTY
FENNEL INFUSION
Take a tablespoon of fennel seeds and place in a cafetiere or teapot. Cover with boiling water and leave to infuse for 3–5 minutes. Drink freely throughout the day. Fennel is a natural diuretic.

invigor8

This is an absolute super juice – a low-calorie, virtually fat-free burst of goodness that will enliven your whole body and help lower blood pressure, aid digestion, boost the immune system and eliminate toxins. If your stress levels have risen to unhealthy heights, this is the best all-round juice you could have, particularly if you are prone to migraines and nausea.

2 medium oranges
$^1/_2$ lemon
100 g (3$^1/_2$ oz) beetroot
100 g (3$^1/_2$ oz) spinach
100 g (3$^1/_2$ oz) celery
100 g (3$^1/_2$ oz) carrot
1 cm ($^1/_2$ inch) cube of fresh root ginger

Peel the orange and lemon, then juice along with the rest of the ingredients. Serve in a pint or two large glasses.

Makes 600 ml (1 pint) or 2 large glasses
Vitamin C 510 mg • Vitamin A 34,736 iu
• Magnesium 164 mg • Folic acid 310 mcg
• Calories 286

day 3

By now you should be feeling **lighter** and **freer** as your body becomes **leaner** and cleaner

You've had two days on the Miracle Juice Diet. A bit daunted by the prospect of another five days and being faced with temptation? Don't worry, it's much easier than you think. If you take a little time in the morning to make the day's juices and store them in airtight flasks, they will be ready for you to enjoy when your willpower weakens.

◄ banana calmer

When you are really up against it and want a quick breakfast or lunch, this smoothie is very high in a wide range of nutrients and is very quick to prepare.

1 small banana
200 ml (7 fl oz) freshly squeezed orange juice
25 g (1 oz) sunflower seeds

Throw all the ingredients into a blender with a couple of ice cubes and process. Serve in a large tumbler and decorate with some strawberries if desired.

Makes 300 ml (10 fl oz) or 1 large glass
Vitamin C 220 mg • Magnesium 113 mg
• Tryptophan 85 mg • Calories 340

on today's menu

start the day
Dandelion and Mint Infusion (page 75)

and then on to
Banana Calmer (page 71)
Deep Breath (page 72)
Hi Tension (page 72)
Power Pack (page 75)
Eye Opener (page 75)

and wind down with
Any herbal tea or infusion of your choice
2 teaspoons flax seeds

snack attack
25 g (1 oz) walnut pieces plus 1 orange

hi tension

Pineapple contains bromelain, an enzyme that aids digestion and is very similar to stomach acid. It is also meant to be highly effective at dissolving blood clots. The only downside is that it is not very kind to tooth enamel and is better if drunk diluted. Celery is the perfect accompaniment as it also aids digestion and lowers blood pressure. This juice is good for re-energizing, detoxifying the liver and replenishing lost fluids.

150 g (5 oz) pineapple
150 g (5 oz) celery
1/2 lemon, peeled

Juice all the ingredients. Serve over ice in a tall glass with some sprigs of fresh mint or fennel.

Makes 200 ml (7 fl oz) or 1 small glass
Vitamin C 33 mg • Magnesium 41 mg • Calories 101

FEEL-GOOD FACTOR

Stress can cause you to hold unnatural tension in every system of your body and has been linked to weight problems. Before you go to bed, destress and detox by taking an Epsom Salt bath. Add a couple of cups of Epsom Salts to your bath water and soak for 15–20 minutes. The magnesium sulphate will draw toxins from the body and sedate the nervous system. You'll sleep like a baby.

deep breath ▶

Quite often if you are stressed you will find that your digestion and circulation are affected, which will leave you feeling fatigued and lacking in energy. Red peppers are excellent at reducing blood pressure and payapa is renowned for its digestive properties.

1 large tomato
100 g (3 1/2 oz) red pepper, deseeded
1/2 papaya – around 125 g (4 oz) – deseeded and peeled

Juice all the ingredients. Blend the juice with a couple of ice cubes in a blender.

Makes 200 ml (7 fl oz) or 1 small glass
Vitamin C 315 mg • Vitamin A 10,851 iu
• Magnesium 51 mg • Calories 124

eye opener

Both carrot and fennel are effective detoxifiers and good for restoring fluid balance because of their high potassium content. Fennel also helps to digest fats, which will give a bit of a hand to your overworked liver. A glass of this juice should give you an immediate lift and ensure that the whites of your eyes are white, not bloodshot.

200 g (7 oz) carrot
200 g (7 oz) fennel

Juice both ingredients and serve in a tall glass over ice with a slice of lemon if desired.

Makes 200 ml (7 fl oz) or 1 small glass
Vitamin A 61,027 iu • Potassium 1,527 mg
• Selenium 3.3 mcg • Calories 152

power pack

Carrots, beetroot and oranges are all high in vitamin C, antioxidants and phytonutrients such as beta-carotene, and are also rich sources of potassium. A great tonic.

250 g (8 oz) carrot
125 g (4 oz) beetroot
1 orange, peeled
125 g (4 oz) strawberries

Juice all of the ingredients together, then pour over ice cubes in a tall glass.

Makes 200 ml (7 fl oz) or 1 small glass
Vitamin C 166 mg • Potassium 1,646 mg
• Magnesium 91 mg • Selenium 5 mcg
• Calories 259

day 4

Smile, because today
is officially your
halfway point

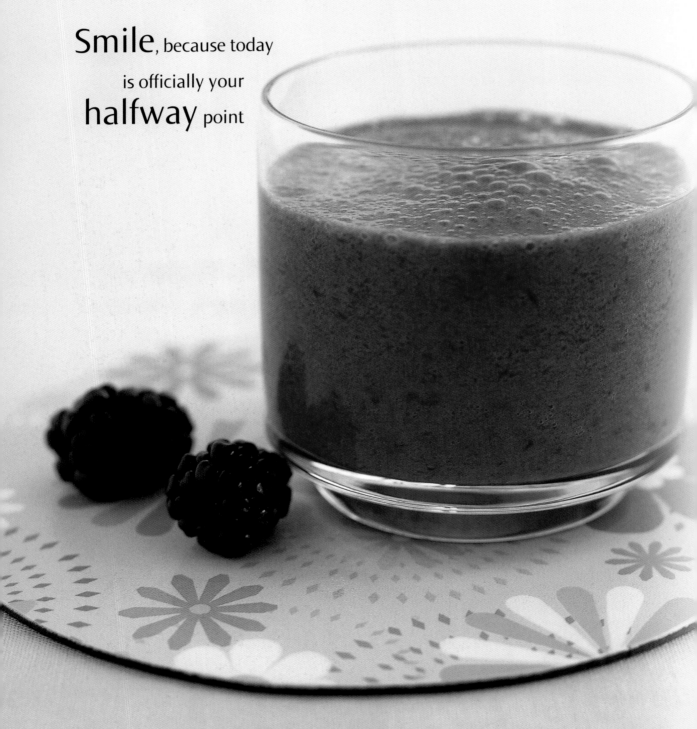

Feeling pretty pleased with yourself? Is it getting a bit easier? You really should be over any headaches or other side effects by now, and feeling more energized and cleaner. If you have a good look in the mirror, the whites of your eyes will be brighter and your skin clearer. Keep going, you're worth it.

◄ grapeberry cream smoothie

Blackberries and purple grapes contain high levels of fluid-balancing potassium and essential bioflavonoids, while the addition of live natural yogurt boosts intestinal flora and calcium intake.

125 g (4 oz) blackberries, fresh or frozen
300 ml (10 fl oz) purple grape juice or 400 g (13 oz) fresh purple grapes, juiced
3 tablespoons natural live yogurt

If using fresh grapes, juice them, then place in the blender with the other ingredients. Process until smooth. Serve immediately.

Makes 350 ml (12 fl oz) or 1 large glass
Vitamin C 20 mg • Potassium 468 mg • Calcium 162 mg • Iron 3.5 mg • Calories 200

on today's menu

start the day
Spicy Orange Tea (page 80)

and then on to
Grapeberry Cream Smoothie (page 77)
Red Rocket (page 78)
Mango Slush (page 78)
Control Freak (page 80)
Mother Nature (page 80)

and wind down with
Any herbal tea or infusion of your choice
2 teaspoons flax seeds

snack attack
25 g (1 oz) Brazil nuts plus 2 kiwifruit

red rocket ▶

Cabbage is a great detoxifier and when combined with the classic juice combination of carrot and apple, is excellent for cleansing the stomach and upper colon.

175 g (6 oz) carrot
250 g (8 oz) apple
125 g (4 oz) red cabbage

Juice all the ingredients and serve over ice with a slice of orange.

Makes 200 ml (7 fl oz) or 1 small glass
Vitamin C 70 mg • Potassium 1,159 mg
• Selenium 3.8 mcg • Calories 250

mango slush

Mangos are an amazing source of beta-carotene, apples are cleansing and cucumber works very effectively as a diuretic. This juice is both highly nourishing and system-clearing.

200 g (7 oz) apple
125 g (4 oz) cucumber
100 g ($3^1/_2$ oz) mango

Juice the apple and cucumber, then blend with the mango and a couple of ice cubes.

Makes 200 ml (7 fl oz) or 1 small glass
Vitamin C 105 mg • Calcium 38 mg • Potassium 56 mg
• Calories 200

control freak

As well as being very high in immune-boosting vitamins A and C, this juice is fantastic for your digestive tract. The sweet potato removes any toxic build-up and will calm inflammation, and the carrot kills bacteria and viruses. So if you have been burning the midnight oil, combined with eating junk food on the run, this is the ideal juice to put you back on track.

150 g (5 oz) sweet potato
2 small oranges, peeled
150 g (5 oz) carrots

Juice all three ingredients and serve over ice, or blend with a couple of ice cubes for a smoother, creamier drink.

Makes 200 ml (7 fl oz) or 1 small glass
Vitamin A 78,357 iu • Vitamin C 200 mg • Calories 358

mother nature

Celery will help to flush out aggravating toxins and rehydrate the system, while the fennel helps to digest fat and will give your liver a break. Grapefruit is a powerful blood cleanser, but don't ever drink with alcohol as it increases its effect.

½ grapefruit, peeled
100 g (3½ oz) celery
100 g (3½ oz) fennel

Juice all the ingredients. Serve in a tall glass over ice. You could add pineapple and tarragon for more variety.

Makes 200 ml (7 fl oz) or 1 small glass
Vitamin C 54 mg • Potassium 729 mg • Folic acid 28 mcg
• Calories 87

LITTLE HOTTY
SPICY ORANGE TEA
Try putting a few slices of orange, a couple of cloves and a couple of star anise in a cafetiere or teapot. Cover with hot water and let infuse for five minutes. Drink freely throughout the day. Alternatively, try Orange Spice herbal teabags.

day 5

Almost there!
Keep up the good work
and feel the benefits

Only three days to go! Keep that willpower going and stay motivated. Try on that special outfit; it should be feeling looser by now. Just think how much better it will fit you if you can manage to stay the distance and finish the whole seven days.

◄ virgin mary smoothie

If you are hankering after a savoury treat, this delicious and filling smoothie will hit the spot. Use fresh tomato juice with no added preservatives for a great boost of lycopene.

50 g (2 oz) red pepper, cored, deseeded and roughly chopped
50 g (2 oz) cucumber, peeled and roughly chopped
25 g (1 oz) spring onion
100 ml (3¹/₂ fl oz) tomato juice
Juice of ¹/₂ lemon
¹/₂ avocado
¹/₂ teaspoon red chilli, deseeded and finely chopped (optional)

Put all the ingredients in a blender and whizz. Season with a little organic tamari sauce if desired.

Makes 300 ml (10 fl oz) or 1 large glass
Vitamin C 91 mg • Vitamin E 4.75 mg • Iron 1.2 mg • Calories 237

on today's menu

start the day
Mint Tea (page 86)

and then on to
Virgin Mary Smoothie (page 83)
Time Out (page 84)
Sharp One (page 84)
Free Flow (page 86)
Pepper Punch (page 86)

and wind down with
Any herbal tea or infusion of your choice
2 teaspoons flax seeds

snack attack
25 g (1 oz) macadamia nuts plus 2 clementines

sharp one

This juice is high in natural sugar, so a great one to reach for if you feel your energy levels dipping; it's also very refreshing on the palate.

2 pears
250 g (8 oz) pineapple
$1/_2$ lime, peeled

Juice all the ingredients and serve over ice cubes.

Makes 300 ml (10 fl oz) or 1 large glass
Calcium 74 mg • Iron 1 mg • Calories 212

time out ▶

If you have been burning the candle at both ends and overloading your system with toxins, give your adrenals a welcome rest and slow down. This juice is packed with ingredients that will act as an effective tonic. Blackberries have a cleansing action on the blood and kiwifruit are an excellent source of vitamin C. The melon is full of beta-carotene and will help rehydrate your entire system.

100 g ($3^1/_2$ oz) cantaloupe melon cubes
100 ($3^1/_2$ oz) blackberries, fresh or frozen
2 kiwifruit, sliced with skins on

Juice all three ingredients. Place in a blender and process with a couple of ice cubes. Pour into a tall glass and serve with a few blackberries if liked.

Makes 250 ml (8 fl oz) or 1 small glass
Vitamin C 215 mg • Vitamin A 4,194 iu
• Magnesium 78 mg • Calories 182

pepper punch

This is a very-fresh tasting juice that is quick and easy to prepare. It is full of beta-carotene and the peppers contain natural silicone, which is a great boost for your skin and nails. Check out the vitamin C content — huge!

100 g (3 ^{1}/$_2$ oz) **each of red, yellow and**
   orange peppers
1 **orange, peeled**
8 **mint leaves, to garnish**

Juice all the ingredients and serve over ice. Stir in the mint leaves.

Makes 200 ml (7 fl oz) or 1 small glass
Vitamin C 333 mg • Selenium 1.5 mcg • Zinc 0.44 mg
• Calories 141

free flow

When we are stressed excess adrenalin causes the blood to thicken, which can have a disastrous impact on health if the stress is prolonged. This smoothie is an excellent blood thinner and balancer as avocado is a good source of vitamin E, which is a highly effective antithrombin, helping to prevent blood coagulation, causing dilation of the blood vessels, allowing the blood to flow more freely towards the heart. It is also vital to pituitary gland function, which ultimately regulates the adrenals.

25 g (1 oz) **watercress**
25 g (1 oz) **spinach**
150 g (5 oz) **celery**
1 **medium apple**
^{1}/$_2$ **small avocado**

Juice the celery, spinach, watercress and apple. Put into a blender with the avocado and a couple of ice cubes and process until smooth. Serve immediately in a tumbler and garnish with a lime slice if liked.

Makes 200 ml (7 fl oz) or 1 small glass
Vitamin C 35 mg • Vitamin E 2.2 mg • Magnesium 70 mg
• Calories 267

day 6

You are within sight of
the finish line so **keep following**
the diet for a **leaner**, healthier life

So, so close to finishing, so don't blow it by cheating now. You can do this, you might even be enjoying it and your body will definitely be thanking you for the break. Keep yourself away from temptation; it will be worth it when you slip into that outfit or those too-tight jeans.

◄ tiger smoothie

Papaya is full of digestive enzymes and is an exceptionally powerful detoxifying fruit. Passion fruit and lime give the smoothie a great zesty taste.

1 orange
$\frac{1}{2}$ lime
1 medium papaya
1 passion fruit

Juice the orange and the lime. Cut the papaya in half and deseed. Put the flesh in a blender along with the passion fruit juice and seeds. Add the juiced orange and lime and a couple of ice cubes. Blend and serve immediately. For a bit of variation, maybe add mango.

Makes 250 ml (8 fl oz) or 1 small glass
Vitamin C 270 mg • Magnesium 25 mg • Calories 135

on today's menu

start the day
Rooibos Tea with Lemon (page 92)

and then on to
Tiger Smoothie (page 89)
Yellow Submarine (page 90)
Melon Berry Juice (page 90)
Blood Brother (page 92)
Super Veggie Boost (page 92)

and wind down with
Any herbal tea or infusion of your choice
2 teaspoons flax seeds

snack attack
25 g (1 oz) pistachio nuts plus 1 raw carrot, cut into sticks

TOP TIP
The nutritional value of nuts and seeds deteriorates very quickly if left in open containers or bags. This is because they have a high oil content, which can easily go rancid if left for a long time. Keep opened packs of nuts in your fridge and nibble regularly.

yellow submarine

Both celery and fennel are effective diuretics and also have appetite-controlling properties.

100 g (3½ oz) celery
100 g (3½ oz) fennel (try parsnip for a change)
75 g (3 oz) pineapple

Juice all three ingredients and serve over ice.

Makes 200 ml (7 fl oz) or 1 small glass
Vitamin C 49 mg • Calcium 115 mg • Calories 144

melon berry juice ▶

There is room for a little flexibility here as it is better to go for fruits that are in season and readily available. Melon is highly hydrating so great after exercise when fluid replacement is a priority.

300 g (10 oz) melon flesh – watermelon, galia, honeydew – whatever is available.
125 g (4 oz) strawberries, raspberries or cherries

Juice both ingredients and serve over ice cubes.

Makes 350 ml (12 fl oz) or 1 large glass
Iron 1.8 mg • Calcium 52 mg • Calories 125

super veggie boost juice ▶

This bright green juice is a fantastic way to benefit from a magnificent seven different vegetables. Sipped slowly it should sustain you and will definitely cleanse your system.

200 g (7 oz) carrot
100 g (3½ oz) green pepper
50 g (2 oz) spinach
50 g (2 oz) onion
100 g (3½ oz) celery
200 g (7 oz) cucumber
100 g (3½ oz) tomato

Juice everything and serve immediately. If you want to vary this, after juicing put in a blender with half an avocado for a power-packed super smoothie.

Makes 200 ml (7 fl oz) or 1 small glass
Vitamin C 210 mg • Potassium 2,130 mg
• Selenium 5 mcg • Iron 5 mg • Calories 230

blood brother

This rich and sweet juice is a great blood restorer and liver regenerator. This is very important because if the liver is overtaxed because of having to deal with harmful substances such as alcohol, it won't be able to effectively cleanse and purify the blood. This will leave the blood full of potentially harmful toxins, which will be circulated around the body.

100 g (3½ oz) red grapes
100 g (3½ oz) beetroot
100 g (3½ oz) plums

Juice all three ingredients and serve over ice cubes.

Makes 200 ml (7 fl oz) or 1 small glass
Vitamin C 15.3 mg • Potassium 611 mg
• Folic acid 51 mcg • Calories 143

LITTLE HOTTY
ROOIBOS TEA WITH LEMON
Rooibos tea is caffeine-free and fantastic if you miss your daily cuppa – try adding a teaspoon of lemon zest or a slice of lemon. You could almost kid yourself you were drinking Earl Grey.

day 7

Well done!
You've made it
to the end

Go and try on that outfit and prance around in front of the mirror. Well done, the last day is here. But remember to be sensible over the coming days. Do you really want to ruin all that hard work by bingeing out? Nobody is expecting you to be a saint, but a little moderation is the key to maintaining your new streamlined figure.

◄ sour red

This is a sharp refreshing juice, ideal for after exercise. If you like your juice a little less sour, substitute the grapefruit for orange and omit the lime.

150 g (5 oz) papaya
150 g (5 oz) grapefruit, peeled
150 g (5 oz) raspberries, fresh or frozen
$^1/_2$ lime

Either juice all the ingredients and serve over ice, or for a variation, juice the grapefruit and lime and whizz in a blender with the papaya and raspberries.

Makes 200 ml (7 fl oz) or 1 small glass
Vitamin C 188 mg • Selenium 4 mcg • Zinc 2 mg
• Calories 193

on today's menu

start the day
Camomile Tea (page 99)

and then on to
Sour Red (page 95)
Green Express (page 96)
Jungle Fever (page 96)
Fast Track (page 99)
Smooth Operator (page 99)

and wind down with
Any herbal tea or infusion of your choice
2 teaspoons flax seeds

snack attack
25 g (1 oz) pine nuts plus 3 celery sticks

green express ▶

A super detoxifier, especially if you've had a few too many cocktails, so bear this in mind should you fall off the rails in the future. Broccoli is one of the greatest all-round foods as it is rich in vitamin C and A, magnesium, folic acid and selenium. It is a great antioxidant and stimulates the liver. Spinach has very high levels of vitamin A, folic acid, magnesium and potassium, and will give the immune system a real kick. Finally apples are superb detoxifiers.

150 g (5 oz) broccoli
2 medium apples
150 g (5 oz) spinach

Juice all three ingredients, alternating the spinach leaves with the broccoli and apple to ensure that the machine doesn't get clogged up with the leaves. It has a green, but very sweet taste, so blend with a couple of ice cubes if desired. Serve in a tall glass.

Makes 200 ml (7 fl oz) or 1 small glass
Vitamin A 18,948 iu • Vitamin C 162 mg
• Magnesium 155 mg • Potassium 1,527 mg
• Selenium 2.5 mcg • Folic acid 270 mcg
• Calories 230

jungle fever

Papaya calms the digestive system, cucumber cools, hydrates and flushes away toxins, and oranges bolster your immune system. With a high potassium content this juice is a great staple when you are trying to lose weight.

125 g (4 oz) papaya
2 oranges
125 g (4 oz) cucumber

Peel and deseed the papaya, and juice along with the oranges and the cucumber. Serve over ice cubes.

Makes 200 ml (7 fl oz) or 1 small glass
Vitamin C 218 mg • Potassium 1,004 mg
• Selenium 2 mcg • Magnesium 51 mg • Calories 184

fast track

Before you pull a face, this juice is surprisingly sweet and a great intestinal cleanser due to the cabbage content.

250 g (8 oz) red cabbage
1 orange, peeled
75 g (3 oz) red grapes

Separate the cabbage into leaves and roughly chop. Juice all three ingredients together and when ready to drink, serve over ice cubes, or whizz in a blender with a couple of ice cubes for a more creamy drink.

Makes 200 ml (7 fl oz) or 1 small glass
Vitamin C 247mg • Calcium 253.75 mg
• Magnesium 48 mg • Iron 1.45 mg
• Calories 302

smooth operator

Bananas are high in tryptophan that is necessary for the production of serotonin, which increases your sense of wellbeing; and as they are high in natural sugars bananas will produce a sense of fullness.

250 g (8 oz) pineapple
1 large carrot
$1/2$ lemon, peeled
2.5 cm (1 inch) cube fresh root ginger
small banana

Juice the pineapple, carrot, lemon and ginger and then blend with the banana and a couple of ice cubes

Makes 200 ml (7 fl oz) or 1 small glass
Vitamin C 61 mg • Calcium 112 mg • Iron 1.75 mg
• Calories 302

LITTLE HOTTY
CAMOMILE TEA

Put 1–2 tablespoons dried camomile flowers in a cafetiere or teapot, cover with boiling water and steep for five minutes. Be aware, this infusion is very calming.

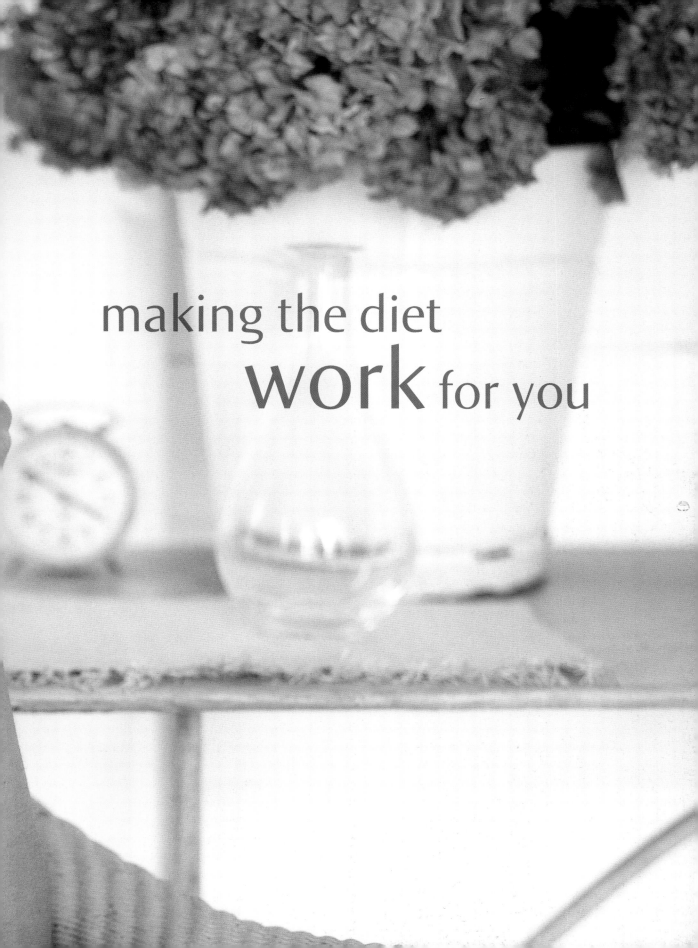

making the diet
work for you

the weekend weight-loss plan

This is the perfect plan if you have a busy lifestyle and have to socialize during the working week. If you followed this suggested routine for one month you could easily lose 3–6 kg (7–14 lb).

Another option is to juice-fast one day a week as a way of maintaining your weight and keeping your system nourished and clean. The weekly menu below will give you an idea of the type of diet you should be following. I have allowed for a little alcohol in the evenings, but ideally you should stick to water and herbal teas.

weekend-only diet plan

	MONDAY	TUESDAY	WEDNESDAY
BREAKFAST	Porridge made with soya milk and 1 fresh apricot and walnuts	Large bowl natural yogurt with mixed berries and flaked almonds	2 poached eggs on 1 slice rye toast with 1 sliced raw tomato
SNACK	Seeds	Apple	Walnuts
LUNCH	Avocado, tuna, onion, lettuce and tomatoes	Chicken salad sandwich	Vegetable soup with wholemeal roll
SNACK	Banana	Seeds	Fresh juice
DINNER	Chicken tandoori with raita and vegetable curry, 1 small beer	Gazpacho, scallops, asparagus and green beans, garlic, 1 glass white wine	Grilled salmon with selection of vegetables, 1 glass rosé

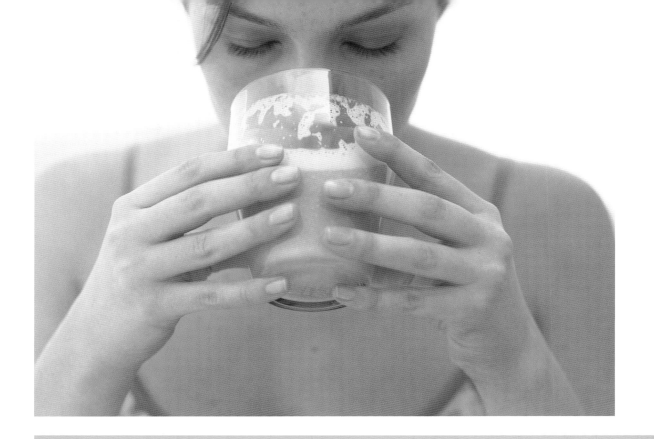

THURSDAY	FRIDAY	SATURDAY	SUNDAY
Sugar-free muesli with fresh strawberries	Any of the Miracle Juice smoothies with 1 apple	Lean Green (page 60) Flat Belly Berry (page 59)	Time Bomb (page 66) Spicy Lemonade (page 69)
Pear	Oatcakes with tahini	Seeds	Macadamia nuts
Roasted vegetables with cod fillet	Grilled sardines with salad	Chilli Orange (page 62)	Ruby Smoothie (page 66)
Orange	Pistachios	Spicy Pear (page 60)	Invigor8 (page 69)
Sashimi, California rolls, miso soup, 2 small glasses sake	Jacket potato filled with guacamole, green salad, 1 glass red wine	Big Red (page 62)	Orange Super Smoothie (page 65)

NB Vary your juice days – choose from days one through seven. Try to stick to one juice from each colour group each day.

the seven-day, one-meal-a-day plan

This approach works brilliantly as it allows you to have lunch with your friends, have a meal (healthy, of course) with your family or partner, or just simply helps you **stay the distance** on a sensible weight-loss programme.

The weight loss will be slower but you could probably stay on this regime for 14 days and then maybe, if you have more weight to lose, replace just one meal a day with a juice or smoothie until you reach your target weight. Do remember though, if you rev up the nutritional value of any banana or avocado-based smoothie with added seeds, flax seeds, a natural live yogurt or wheat germ, you really do have an excellent meal replacement.

the one-meal-a-day plan

	MONDAY	TUESDAY	WEDNESDAY
JUICE 1	Flat Belly Berry (page 59)	Ruby Smoothie (page 66)	Banana Calmer (page 71)
SNACK	Seeds	Apple	Walnuts
JUICE 2	Chilli Orange (page 62)	Invigor8 (page 69)	Eye Opener (page 75)
JUICE 3	Big Red or Lean Green (page 62 or 60)	Orange Super Smoothie or Time Bomb (page 65 or 66)	Power Pack or Hi Tension (page 75 or 72)
LUNCH OR DINNER	Quorn or tofu marinated with tamari sauce, ginger and sesame oil, stir-fried with selection of vegetables	Salmon on bed of wilted spinach with sweet potato mash	Chunky tomato and vegetable soup with haricot beans

THURSDAY	FRIDAY	SATURDAY	SUNDAY
Grapeberry Cream Smoothie (page 77)	Sharp One (page 84	Tiger Smoothie (page 89)	Smooth Operator (page 99)
Pear	2 clementines	Pumpkin seeds	Carrot and celery sticks
Control Freak (page 80)	Time Out (page 84)	Blood Brother (page 92)	Green Express (page 96)
Mango Slush or Mother Nature (page 78 or 80)	Free Flow or Virgin Mary Smoothie (page 86 or 83)	Super Boost Juice or Yellow Submarine (page 92 or 90)	Sour Red or Jungle Fever (page 95 or 96)
Prawn and lentil curry with brown rice and spinach	Bowl of quorn chilli served with iceberg lettuce	Chicken breast poached in stock and fresh tarragon served with broccoli and carrots	Either tinned or fresh tuna and avocado salad with rocket, spring onions and cherry tomatoes

NB Remember with both these adaptations, you should still avoid caffeine, refined carbohydrates and processed foods, minimize salt in-take, drink plenty of water and stick to the exercise routine previously recommended.

keeping the weight off

By now you've managed to lose up to 3 kg (7 lb) in seven days.
Wouldn't it be **nice** to **not** have to do anything so drastic ever again?

Coming down from the diet

Before we deal with that topic, let's get you through the first couple of days after the diet. I would suggest reintroducing solid food carefully.

On the first day after the diet

Breakfast Have either a small bowl porridge with a little fresh fruit, a natural live yogurt with chopped pear and walnuts, or if you like, one of the smoothies with added psyllium or flax seeds.

Snack Have either a handful of seeds or a banana.

Lunch Try steamed vegetables with brown rice, drizzled with sesame oil and tamari dressing.

Snack Have either a juice or some crudités with tahini dip.

Dinner Try a large salad with avocado and sunflower seeds.

On the second day after the diet

Breakfast Eat two poached eggs on rye toast or one of the above options.

Snack Natural live yogurt with honey and berries makes a nutritious snack.

Lunch Baked sweet potato with tomato and onion salad will fill the lunchtime gap.

Snack A juice or smoothie will help you over the mid-afternoon slump in energy.

Dinner A grilled salmon steak with broccoli and green beans is a healthy option.

If you follow the rules outlined in the preparation phase of the diet, combined with regular exercise you'll stay trim. If you do succumb to the odd few glasses of wine or bar of chocolate, simply replace a couple of meals with a delicious and healthy juice or smoothie to get you back on the right track.

I still need to lose more weight

Look at the two alternative systems and pick either the One-meal-a-day Plan or the Weekend Weight-loss Plan. This will allow you to carry on losing weight while still getting the correct balance of nutrients to keep you fit and healthy. Long-term weight control and good health depend on the following:

Waving goodbye to:
* Refined carbohydrates and processed foods
* Fizzy drinks, sugary cordials and commercially prepared juices
* Caffeine-laden coffee and tea
* Hydrogenated and trans fats; don't fry food
* Salty snacks and overly salted food
* Sedentary lifestyle

Continuing with:
* Wholegrains and pulses
* Plenty of fresh fruits and vegetables; aim to eat at least 50 per cent raw and rev up your phyto-nutrient quota by having a daily power-packed juice
* High-quality protein – lean poultry and game, organic meat, fish and shellfish, free-range eggs and occasional small portions cheese
* Natural live yogurt
* Healthy cold-pressed oils such as olive, flax seed and hemp
* Herbal teas and plenty of water
* Limited alcohol consumption – ideally the occasional glass of organic red wine
* Continue to take supplements for optimum health
* 30 minutes of cardiovascular exercise and stretching daily
* Strengthening routine at least three times per week

eating out & socializing

Having a **meal out** need not be a problem,
just don't be afraid to ask **questions** and state your preferences –
restaurants are used to this.

basic guidelines

* Be careful with commercial salad dressing, maybe opt for lemon juice and olive oil instead.
* Say no to croutons and the bread basket.
* Ask for your main course to be grilled, steamed or poached. Bulk up by asking for extra portions of vegetables or a side salad.

* Have water with your meal and don't add loads of hidden calories by consuming high levels of alcohol – a large glass of wine is around 100 kcals.
* If you are going to go out for a meal, certain types of restaurants are better than others – in general avoid fast-food outlets.
* Food is better eaten slowly and digested properly.

good menu choices

RESTAURANT	STARTER	MAIN	VEGETABLES
ITALIAN	Antipasto plate, grilled calamari, prawns in garlic, prosciutto with Parmesan, carpaccio	Grilled chicken, fish, steak, veal cutlets, chicken piccata	Salad, courgettes, aubergine, peppers
INDIAN	Chicken tikka, tandoori chicken or prawns	Most curries with meat or fish but limit potatoes and rice, spinach with paneer. No naan bread or poppadums	Cucumber raita, salad
CHINESE (Ask for no sugar or MSG in sauces)	Chicken or prawn satay	Steamed fish or Peking duck without pancakes	Stir-fries with mangetout, ginger, bean sprouts, bok choy
JAPANESE	Sashimi (raw fish), miso soup	Meat or fish Teppenyaki, tofu	Grilled vegetables
SPANISH	Gazpacho, mushrooms in garlic, fresh anchovies, prawns, scallops wrapped in bacon	Grilled fish, squid, meat – don't load up on paella	Big mixed salads, green beans with garlic
THAI	Tom Ka Khai (chicken soup with coconut, or ask for it to be made with prawns)	Most curries made with coconut and fresh Thai curry pastes – ask for no sugar to be added	Amazing salads with a spicy kick – watch out for added noodles
FRENCH	Asparagus (ask for lemon and oil rather than Hollandaise), steamed mussels, oysters	Poached salmon, Bouillabaisse, chicken, grilled steak or lamb	Mixed vegetables or green salad
GREEK	Olives, tzatziki with crudités	Souvla, kleftiko, chicken kebabs	Greek salad with feta

index

a

actinidin 20
adenosine 46
adrenaline 46
alcohol 47, 51
allyl sulphide 19
alpha-carotene 19
amino acids 12
anthocyanins 19
apples 21
  Flat Belly Berry 59
  Free Flow 86
  Green Express 96
  Lean Green 60
  Mango Slush 78
  Red Rocket 78
  Ruby Smoothie 66
  Spicy Lemonade 69
apricots, Orange Super Smoothie 65
arm circles 36
attitudes, changing 49
avocados 21
  face mask 84
  Free Flow 86
  Virgin Mary Smoothie 83

b

back raises 41
bacteria, intestinal ('friendly') 20, 25
bananas 20
  Banana Calmer 71
  Orange Super Smoothie 65
  Smooth Operator 99
beetroot
  Blood Brother 92
  Invigor8 69
  Power Pack 75
belly dancing 32
berries 20
beta-carotene 19
bicep curl 37
Big Red 62
bioflavonoids 21
blackberries
  Grapeberry Cream Smoothie 77
  Time Out 84
blenders 52
Blood Brother 92
blueberries, Flat Belly Berry 59
Body Mass Index (BMI) 28–9

brewer's yeast 27
broccoli 22
  Green Express 96
  Lean Green 60
  Time Bomb 66
bromelain 21

c

cabbage 22
caffeine 46, 51
calf raises 38
calf stretch 35
calories 10
Camomile Tea 99
cancer 15, 18
carbohydrates 46, 48
carcinogens 18
carotenoids 21, 22
carrots 23
  Chilli Orange 62
  Control Freak 80
  Eye Opener 75
  Invigor8 69
  Orange Super Smoothie 65
  Power Pack 75
  Red Rocket 78
  Smooth Operator 99
  Super Veggie Boost Juice 92
celery 23
  Free Flow 86
  Hi Tension 72
  Invigor8 69
  Mother Nature 80
  Spicy Pear 60
  Super Veggie Boost Juice 92
  Yellow Submarine 90
chest press 36
chilli
  Chilli Orange 62
  Virgin Mary Smoothie 83
cholesterol 15, 47
citrus fruit 21
colon 15
Control Freak 80
cortisol 46
coumarins 19
cranberries 21
cranberry juice, Flat Belly Berry 59
cucumbers
  Jungle Fever 96
  Lean Green 60
  Mango Slush 78
  Super Veggie Boost Juice 92
  Virgin Mary Smoothie 83
cycling 32

d

daily workout 34–41
dancing 32
Dandelion and Mint Infusion 75
Deep Breath 72
degenerative diseases 14
detoxification 14, 44
diabetes 51
diet
  daily 96
  Mediterranean 18
  one-meal-a-day plan 104–5
  preparation 44, 48
  week (days 1-7) 58–99
  weekend weight-loss plan 102–3
digestion 10
doctors 29
dopamine 46

e

eating out 108–9
energy levels 51
enzymes 12
Epsom Salt bath 72
equipment 52–3
exercise 6
  daily workout 34–41
  fitness (fit bit) 62, 66, 75, 78, 84, 90, 99
  ideas 32–3
Eye Opener 75

f

face mask 84
Fast Track 99
fat 10
fat-soluble vitamins 16
fats 47, 48–9
fatty acids 48
fennel 23
  Eye Opener 75
  Mother Nature 80
  Yellow Submarine 90
Fennel Infusion 69
fibre 12
fish liver oils 25–6
Flat Belly Berry 59
flavonoids 19
flax seeds 12, 24, 26
food, reintroduction 6, 106
food processing 46
Free Flow 86
fruit 18, 20–2, 48

g

gardening 32
garlic 27
ginger 27
    Invigor8 69
    Smooth Operator 99
    Spicy Lemonade 69
    Spicy Pear 60
glucarase 19
glutathione 21
goals 96
Grapeberry Cream Smoothie 77
grapefruits 21
    Mother Nature 80
    Sour Red 95
grapes
    Blood Brother 92
    Fast Track 99
    Grapeberry Cream Smoothie 77
Green Express 96
green leafy vegetables 23

h

health problems 29
healthy fats 48–9
Hi Tension 72
hunger pangs 86
hydrogenated fats 47

i

immune system 51
indoles 19, 22
infusions
    Camomile Tea 99
    Dandelion and Mint 75
    Fennel 69
    Lemon and Ginger 62
    Mint Tea 86
    Rooibos Tea with Lemon 92
    Spicy Orange Tea 80
ingredients 55
Invigor8 69
isoflavones 19

j

jogging 32
juicers 52
juices
    benefits 12
    commercial 12
    drinking 60
    water content 10
juicing 52
Jungle Fever 96
junk food 46, 51

k

kidneys 10
kiwifruit 20
    Lean Green 60
    Time Out 84
knee pull 34

l

Lean Green 60
lecithin 21
leg raises 39
Lemon and Ginger Infusion 62
lemons 21
    Hi Tension 72
    Invigor8 69
    Lemon and Ginger Infusion 62
    Smooth Operator 99
    Spicy Lemonade 69
    Virgin Mary Smoothie 83
lignan precursors 19
lignans 24
limes 21
    Chilli Orange 62
    Sharp One 84
    Tiger Smoothie 89
limonene 19
linoleic acid 48
linolenic acid 48
liver 10, 15
lower leg raises 39
lutein 19
lycopene 19, 22

m

mangos 22
    Mango Slush 78
mannose 21
martial arts 32
Mediterranean diet 18
melons 20
    Melon Berry Juice 90
    Time Out 84
milk thistle 26
minerals 12, 16
mint
    Dandelion and Mint Infusion 75
    Mint Tea 86
Mother Nature 80
motivation 50–1

n

nutrients 10, 12
nuts 27, 89

o

obesity 26, 28
omega-3 25–6, 48
omega-6 48
one-meal-a-day plan 104–5
onions, Super Veggie Boost Juice 92
orange juice, Banana Calmer 71
oranges 21
    Control Freak 80
    Fast Track 99
    Invigor8 69
    Jungle Fever 96
    Orange Super Smoothie 65
    Pepper Punch 86
    Power Pack 75
    Ruby Smoothie 66
    Spicy Orange Tea 80
    Tiger Smoothie 89

p

P-coumaric acid 19
papain 21
papaya 21
    Deep Breath 72
    Jungle Fever 96
    Sour Red 95
    Tiger Smoothie 89
passion fruits, Tiger Smoothie 89
pears
    Sharp One 84
    Spicy Pear 60
pectin 20
pectoral stretch 35
peppers 23
    Deep Breath 72
    Pepper Punch 86
    Spicy Lemonade 69
    Super Veggie Boost Juice 92
    Virgin Mary Smoothie 83
phenols 21
phytonutrients 12, 18–19
pilates 33
pineapples 21
    Chilli Orange 62
    Hi Tension 72
    Lean Green 60
    Sharp One 84
    Smooth Operator 99
    Yellow Submarine 90
plums 21
    Blood Brother 92
polyphenols 19
potassium 20, 22
Power Pack 75
power walking 32

prebiotics 20
preparations 6, 44
probiotic ('friendly') bacteria 20, 25
protein 48
psyllium 12, 25
pumpkin seeds 26
push-ups 37

r
raspberries
    Ruby Smoothie 66
    Sour Red 95
red cabbage
    Fast Track 99
    Red Rocket 78
refined carbohydrates 46
Rooibos Tea with Lemon 92
Ruby Smoothie 66

s
salt 47
science 10
seeds 26, 89
sesame seeds 26
Sharp One 84
shopping 27, 55
side curls 40
side effects, detoxification 44
side reaches 34
side-to-side 41
silicones 23
silymarin see milk thistle
sit-ups 40
skipping 32
Smooth Operator 99
socializing 108
Sour Red 95

soya 26
Spicy Lemonade 69
Spicy Orange Tea 80
Spicy Pear 60
spinach
    Free Flow 86
    Green Express 96
    Invigor8 69
    Super Veggie Boost Juice 92
    Time Bomb 66
spring cleaning 92
squats, wide 38
strawberries
    Big Red 62
    Melon Berry Juice 90
    Power Pack 75
    Ruby Smoothie 66
sugar 51
sulphoraphanes 19
sunflower seeds 26
    Banana Calmer 71
super foods 24–7
Super Veggie Boost Juice 92
supplements 16, 24–7
sweet potatoes 22
    Control Freak 80
swimming 32

t
teeth, brushing 78
television 80
thermogenesis 24
thigh stretch 35
Tiger Smoothie 89
Time Bomb 66
Time Out 84
tomato juice, Virgin Mary Smoothie

83
tomatoes 22
    Big Red 62
    Deep Breath 72
    Super Veggie Boost Juice 92
    Time Bomb 66
toxins 6, 10, 14, 44
trace elements 16
trans fats 47
tricep stretch 35

u
upper leg raises 39

v
vegetables 18, 20, 22–3, 48
Virgin Mary Smoothie 83
vitamins 12, 16

w
walking 32
wardrobe makeover 69
water 49
water-soluble vitamins 16
watercress, Free Flow 86
weekend weight-loss plan 102–3
weight 28
    loss 6, 54, 106
wide squats 38
workout, daily 34–41

y
Yellow Submarine 90
yogurt 25
    Grapeberry Cream Smoothie 77
    Ruby Smoothie 66

acknowledgements

Executive Editor Nicola

Editor Emma Pattison

Executive Art Editor Penny Stock

Senior Production Controller Manjit Sihra

Photographer Janine Hosegood

Stylist Rachel Jukes

Model Bailee Roup

Home Economists Mary Wall and Carol Tennant

The author and publisher would like to thank PPL (tel 01159 608646, www.superjuicer.co.uk) for the loan of their Superjuicer, and www.ukjuicers.com for the loan of their juicer.